Newsletters Now: From Classic to New Wave

Newsletters Now:

From Classic to New Wave

Steven Heller & Elinor Pettit

Library of Applied Design
An Imprint of
PBC International, Inc.

Distributor to the book trade in the United States and Canada

Rizzoli International Publications Inc.

300 Park Avenue South

New York, NY 10010

Distributor to the art trade in the United States and Canada

PBC International, Inc.

One School Street

Glen Cove, NY 11542

Distributor throughout the rest of the world

Hearst Books International

1350 Avenue of the Americas

New York, NY 10019

Library of Congress Cataloging–in–Publication Data

Heller, Steven.

Newsletters now : from classic to new wave / by Steven Heller and Elinor Pettit.

    p.   cm.

  Includes index.

  ISBN 0–86636–338–6 (alk. paper). — ISBN 0-86636-431-5 (alk. paper)

  1. Printing, Practical—Layout. 2. Newsletters—Design.

  3. Graphic arts. I. Pettit, Elinor I. Pettit, Elinor. II. Title.

Z246.H45 1996   95-12990

686.2 ' 252—dc20   CIP

CAVEAT– Information in this text is believed accurate, and will pose no
problem for the student or casual reader. However, the author was often
constrained by information contained in signed release forms, information
that could have been in error or not included at all. Any misinformation
(or lack of information) is the result of failure in these attestations.
The author has done whatever is possible to insure accuracy.

Color separation by Fine Arts Repro House Co., LTD., Hong Kong

Printing and binding by Dai Nippon Printing Group

Design by Mirko Ilić

Photography by Naum Kazhdan unless otherwise noted.

PRINTED IN HONG KONG

10 9 8 7 6 5 4 3 2 1

Table of Contents

Newsletters

It is not known when the first newsletter was published or by whom. However, it is reasonable to assume that the practice of including news in letters is as old as the letter itself. But the newsletter as we know it today probably did not begin until the late-nineteenth or early-twentieth century when large businesses entered the early stages of corporate communications. The newsletter was born of a need to transmit newsworthy business information on a large scale to more recipients than was possible through a mere letter. Advances in printing and mail delivery made inexpensive production and accelerated distribution feasible. So newsletters, a curious cross between a newspaper and a form letter, suggested a kind of informal formality.

The earliest known newsletters were actually two- or four-page letters folded into standard envelopes. Although composed on a typewriter, often on the letterhead of the business or organization that issued it, the information was prioritized in pyramid newspaper fashion. A typewritten headline announced the main topic and subheads identified secondary stories or items. Ring binder holes were often punched out of the left hand margin to encourage recipients to save the missives. But for the most part, newsletters were as ephemeral as newspapers; so few of the early ones have survived.

The contemporary newsletter, with its formally designed masthead or logo and typeset text, began after World War II when corporate communications developed to meet the needs of growing multinational businesses. Increased activity in the world's economic markets necessitated that all publicly held companies issue annual reports and/or other periodic correspondence to their stockholders. To facilitate this task, many large corporations engaged graphic designers to develop and maintain their business identity programs. The leading corporate designers of the day, among them Paul Rand, Lester Beall, and Brownjohn, Chermayeff & Geismar, created consistent visual personalities which were affixed to everything from corporate letterheads, to packages, to vehicles. Also developed were more efficient means to communicate with subsidiaries, employees, customers, and investors. The newsletter was one of the most efficient.

Compared to a newspaper or magazine, a newsletter required less of everything: pages, type, pictures, color, and, most importantly, labor. A newsletter could be printed on small presses in fewer quantities, at less time, effort, and cost than almost any other printed instrument. Producing a newsletter further required reduced, or often no editorial or design staffs. In the scheme of official communications the newsletter was the least complicated and most streamlined informational document a business could employ. No wonder by the 1950s it was adopted for various in- and out-of-house publishing by most corporations. Soon nonprofit organizations, for whom inexpensive communication was not a choice but a requisite, adopted the newsletter to announce programs, report on events, finances, and otherwise provide an alternative to expensive

No excuse for bad design

annual reports or other magazine-like publications.

The newsletter requires very low maintenance. Before the advent of computer desktop publishing, the commercial printer usually provided an unpretentious layout which was strictly adhered to from issue to issue. The newsletter was either given away to a fixed number of recipients or sold by subscription so as to avoid costly overruns. In fact, so large was the economic saving that some financially marginal publishers only used the newsletter medium: *I.F. Stone's Weekly*, one of the most famous "alternative newsletters," reported on Washington politics for over twenty years before its editor, Izzy Stone, retired in the 1980s. And a similar biweekly "investigative newsletter," *The Washington Spectator*, continues to publish to this day much in the same form as it has been for twenty years.

For a long time, the standards of the postal service required that all newsletters were essentially the same format: a standard letter sized (8½" x 11") sheet either printed on two sides or a double letter (11" x 17") folded in half, resulting in four pages. The more ambitious newsletters might include an extra double letter sized sheet for a total of eight pages. Sometimes these "signatures" were stapled (or stitched) together, while other times they were folded and gathered. For mailing purposes they were additionally folded into horizontal thirds to either fit into a standard envelope or be mailed without an envelope. Nothing could be easier.

But from a design point of view, few media were as predictable. Despite the newsletter's benefits, most were visually mundane. The basic form did not allow for—and most clients did not encourage—a loosening of strictures. Newsletters required squeezing the most information into the smallest space. They were functional, not creative. Moreover, when designers were involved, newsletters were virtually ignored after the first issues were formatted, and layouts were left to job printers or secretaries. This was common practice until the 1960s when staid visual media were being routinely challenged by an exuberant graphic eclecticism that was influencing the practice of all design.

Although the newsletter was not generally one of the first print media to be reevaluated, graphic designers eventually began to freely play and experiment with its form, particularly when it was a component of a larger communications system.

New, jazzier approaches included vivacious mastheads and logos, variegated grids, splashy type treatments, conceptual illustrations, and often the introduction of "editorial" color in artwork, photographs, type, as well as color tints over sidebars and pull quotes. The basic size and shape was also up for grabs. By the 1970s newsletters were no longer restricted to letter sizes alone, but included tabloids (or newspaper sized sheets), squares, long narrow verticals, in fact, whatever size and shape that was workable and affordable. Various folding methods, including accordion and gatefold, increased the options. A variety of paperstocks—from matte to glossy—enhanced tactility. In some cases even the routinely tight production budgets increased so that the newsletter might appear more like a magazine. The newsletter no longer had to be drab or commonplace. In fact, since most newsletters are not encumbered by paid advertising, the four, six, eight or more pages could be freely designed within the limits of the content itself.

Yet despite reinvention and reappreciation, the newsletter is still fraught with several problems. Many companies and organizations use newsletters as the most direct means of communications, but curiously do not adhere to principles of good design. Where graphic designers are not involved, newsletters are laid out in a tedious or, in the argot of computers, default manner. While the personal computer with its design programs has allowed the layman to create more "professional" looking newsletters, it has also contributed to visual redundancy. The so-called foolproof design template(s) is merely a tool. Like filling an empty room, although it has sturdy walls and sound floors, it takes someone with taste and talent to make it attractive, no less exciting. Without a graphic designer's eye (and intuition), a newsletter can be as visually uninteresting, and certainly as uninspired, as that empty room.

A generic newsletter template may come equipped with standard fixtures—masthead, columns, headline type. It may even include a few extras—a pull-quote style, initial caps, decorative rules—but without a knowing hand and keen eye these are merely unsolved puzzle pieces. The designer knows how to best compose these elements, but further determines what added ingredients—illustration, photo, type treatment—are necessary to transcend the generic mediocrity.

Nevertheless, the fact that a graphic designer is designing a newsletter does not insure virtuosity either. Even some of the most professionally designed newsletters exhibit a production-line quality. Sure, newsletters are not generally designed to be redesigned from issue to issue, but a good format, no matter how consistent, should not be lifeless. A good format is a structure that encourages variety, if not play. Today's newsletters fit into four qualitative categories. Please note that the first two do not appear in this book: 1. Poorly (or unprofessionally) designed (usually by a non-designer); 2. Unimaginatively designed (either by a non-designer or designer following some generic format); 3. Professionally designed (usually by a designer adhering to a distinctive but consistent format); 4. Adventurously designed (also by a designer, but sometimes by a talented amateur, testing the limits of graphic presentation). Those in the last two categories fit into the following genres: 1. Classical, often typographically driven where consistent combinations of two or more traditionally elegant typefaces define the visual personality of the newsletter. In this genre different color schemes or illustrations break the consistent format; 2. Post-Modern, often a marriage of type and image—of tradition and contemporenity—where au courant color and decorative design schemes are used to bolster the visual impact. Unlike classical, the post-modern approach is purposefully timely, and may be subject to redesign more often; 3. New Wave, despite the basic limitations of newsletters, those included in this genre are wild, crazy and playful. Following the current edgy standards, these use type as much for texture as text, and rely on printing tricks and gimmicks to enhance the message. Indeed some of these newsletters not only change format from issue to issue, but size and shape, too.

The examples in *Newsletters Now* represent all these "creative" categories and genres, from the sublime to the ridiculous, from the legible to the cautiously illegible, yet nonetheless comprehensible. With so many functional and aesthetic options to choose from there is little excuse for even the most routine newsletter to appear dull. Whether the job calls for corporate conservatism or cultural eclecticism, the range of potential forms and formats is anything but constricting. The goal of this book is to demonstrate to both designers and users of newsletters (or kindred desktop publishing instruments) that this medium is as free as the client allows and the creator decides. There can be no excuse for anything less.

—Steven Heller

section l

AIGA WASHINGTON
CHAPTER
QUARTERLY
JOURNAL

c l i e n t

AMERICAN INSTITUTE
OF GRAPHIC
ARTS/WASHINGTON
CHAPTER

b u s i n e s s

GRAPHIC ARTS
ASSOCIATION

d e s i g n   f i r m

PAT TAYLOR, INC.

d e s i g n e r

PAT TAYLOR

This booklet-styled newsletter is a masterpiece of conceptual design. The cover
of each issue is printed in a
different flat color and illustrated with one of four communications codes that
spells out AIGA.

pages 16, frequency
Quarterly, quantity 900,
typography Photographic
Typesetting

AMERICAN INSTITUTE OF GRAPHIC ARTS/WASHINGTON CHAPTER   WINTER 1991

CHICAIGAO

client

AMERICAN INSTITUTE
OF GRAPHIC
ARTS/CHICAGO
CHAPTER

business

GRAPHIC ARTS
ASSOCIATION

design firm

CROSBY ASSOCIATES
INC.

art director

BART CROSBY

designer

CARL WOHLT

illustrator

WILL NORTHERNER

The tabloid newsletter not
only increases the size of
editorial real estate, but
allows for splashy presentation. This issue is typo-
graphically elegant in its
newsy appearance.

pages 22, frequency
Biannually, quantity 5,000,
software QuarkXPress

CHICAIGAO

AIGA in Chicago

A publication of the Chicago Chapter, the American Institute of Graphic Arts.

Summer 1990

Taking Different Roads to the Future:
Design and the Creative Process
AIGA in Chicago *explores the distinct paths being pursued by designers, as well as the unifying role played by the creative process.*

CHIC AIGA O

![AIGA in Chicago — horizontal black bar]

AIGA in Chicago *A publication of the Chicago Chapter, the American Institute of Graphic Arts*

Winter 1993/Issue 14 **For the Public Good**
Designers are passionate about pro bono work.
We examine how—and why—the torch keeps burning.

CHICAIGO
client
AMERICAN INSTITUTE
OF GRAPHIC
ARTS/CHICAGO
CHAPTER
design firm
LISKA AND
ASSOCIATES, INC.
art director
STEVE LISKA
designer
MARCOS CHAVEZ
illustrator
CHUCK GONZALES

A graphic design organization should have well-
designed printed materials,
but more importantly, this
tabloid newsletter's typography does not overpower its
content with fancy designer
tricks or gimmicks.

pages 16-28, frequency
Varies, quantity Varies,
software QuarkXPress

AIGA MINNESOTA
ISSUES

client

AMERICAN INSTITUTE
OF GRAPHIC
ARTS/MINNESOTA
CHAPTER

business

GRAPHIC ARTS
ASSOCIATION

designer/
illustrator

STUART FLAKE

The average newsletter reader may not appreciate the subtleties in design from one designer to the next, but the recipients of a design organization's publications will certainly notice. Nevertheless, comparing different approaches can be instructive for all.

pages Foldout, frequency Monthly, quantity 800, software QuarkXPress, Adobe Illustrator

THE NATURE OF DESIGN ONCE AGAIN THE TIME HAS COME TO REGISTER FOR DESIGN CAMP. THIS YEAR'S CONFERENCE WILL TAKE PLACE ON OCTOBER 7, 8 AND 9 AT RUTTGER'S BAY LAKE RESORT IN THE BEAUTIFUL NORTH WOODS OF MINNESOTA. YOU HAVE BEEN TEASED AND THE REGISTRATION MATERIALS ARE PROBABLY IN THAT PILE ON YOUR DESK. WELL, WE WANT TO TEASE SOME MORE—TWIST THAT ARM A LITTLE—BECAUSE THIS IS ONE DESIGN CAMP YOU DON'T WANT TO MISS!

THIS YEAR'S DESIGN CAMP COMMITTEE INCLUDES APPROXIMATELY 20 VOLUNTEERS. OUR FIRST AND MOST IMPORTANT JOB WAS TO SELECT THE MAIN SPEAKERS: TWO DESIGNERS, AN ILLUSTRATOR, A PHOTOGRAPHER AND AN "OTHER." FROM A LIST OF OVER 100 NAMES OUR COMMITTEE ARRIVED AT THESE FIVE WELL-RESPECTED PROFESSIONALS:

- REBECCA MENDEZ'S WORK IS MORE THAN DESIGN—IT'S ABOUT BODY AND SOUL.
- DAVID CARSON HAS BEEN CALLED A "MASTER OF TYPOGRAPHY" BY *GRAPHICS* MAGAZINE, AND HE'S A VERY CONTROVERSIAL FIGURE IN THE DESIGN WORLD.
- BRAD HOLLAND HAS ELUDED OUR LURE FOR THE PAST COUPLE YEARS BUT WE FINALLY CAUGHT HIM. AN INTERNATIONALLY CELEBRATED ILLUSTRATOR, BRAD WILL DEFINITELY BE WORTH THE WAIT.
- LAURIE KRATOCHVIL (RHYMES WITH ROCKVILLE). LIKE HER PHOTO DIRECTION FOR *ROLLING STONE* MAGAZINE, IS BEST DESCRIBED AS ROCK-AND-ROLL.
- STEPHEN SIDELINGER IS THE "OTHER." TOSS THOSE ANNUALS—YOU'LL FIND YOUR OWN VISUAL LANGUAGE.

OUR SECOND HURDLE WAS TO CONFIRM THE WORKSHOPS. THEY INCLUDE GETTING LOST (AND FOUND) IN THE GREAT OUTDOORS, AS WELL AS LEARNING SOMETHING WHILE INDOORS.

WITH SPEAKERS AND WORKSHOPS CONFIRMED, IT'S GAME TIME. SOCIALIZE WITH YOUR FELLOW CAMPERS WHILE GOING ON A SCAVENGER HUNT, TYING A KNOT, STARTING A FIRE, SHOOTING ARROWS AND JUMPING IN THE LAKE (WITH A CANOE, OF COURSE). OTHER ACTIVITIES INCLUDE VOLLEYBALL, BOCCE BALL, SOFTBALL AND GOLF.

WHEN THE SUN GOES DOWN WE WILL DANCE THE NIGHT AWAY TO THAT ROCKABILLY SOUND OF JACK KNIFE AND THE SHARPS.

THAT'S THE SCOOP. YOU DON'T HAVE ANY EXCUSES—WE'VE HEARD THEM ALL (WELL, MOST OF THEM). ALL WE HAVE TO SAY TO THAT IS BLAH BLAH BLAH. THE BOTTOM LINE IS YOU'LL DEFINITELY LEARN SOMETHING NEW, YOU'LL MEET SOME OF YOUR PEERS AND IT'S A GREAT TIME TO GET AWAY. DON'T FORGET THAT REGISTRATION IS LIMITED AND THE DEADLINE IS SEPTEMBER 9. ANY QUESTIONS? CALL ANDY POWELL AT 349-6611 OR GERI THOMPSON (507) 663-5428. THE DESIGN OF NATURE

ANDY POWELL, DESIGN CAMP CO-CHAIR

KNOCK 'EM DEAD AT DESIGN CAMP Remember summer camp? Canoe races, that cute tennis pro, your first kiss (or so you told everyone at school) and, of course, those classic practical jokes on your friends, enemies and bunkmates. Bring a little of that old Camp Chequamegon spirit back, design-style, with these ideas for practical jokes for your unsuspecting Design Camp-mates.

REPEATEDLY ASK THE *ROLLING STONE* PHOTO EDITOR IF SHE KNOWS MICK.

REPLACE THE LABELS ON THE EXPENSIVE BEER WITH A LIKENESS OF THE SCHLITZ MALT LIQUOR BULL.

SECRETLY REPLACE THE FINE COFFEE RUTTGER'S USUALLY SERVES WITH DARK, SPARKLING FOLGER'S CRYSTALS.

GLUE YOUR NEIGHBOR'S ART SUPPLIES INTO YOUR OWN PIECE DURING THE COLLAGE SEMINAR.

TAKE THE ARROW OUT OF YOUR BOSS'S COMPASS BEFORE THE ORIENTEERING EXERCISES. FROM A SAFE DISTANCE, LAUGH HEARTILY WHEN THE SEARCH PARTY RETURNS HER OR HIM TO CAMP SUNBURNED AND DEHYDRATED.

WEAR YOUR [illegible] SWEATSHIRT TO REBECCA MENDEZ'S LECTURE.

DURING THE DIGITAL INFORMATION SEMINAR, USE A STACK OF COATED PAPER IN LIEU OF A FOLDING CHAIR.

ASK FELLOW CAMPERS IF THEY'RE GOING TO ATTEND THE WORKSHOP ON NUDE PRESS CHECKS.

USE THIS QUERY ON THE *RAYGUN* DIRECTOR: "HOW DO I KNOW IF THE COLOR BLUE IS THE SAME TO YOU AS IT IS TO ME?"

AT RANDOM TIMES DURING GROUP OUTINGS, TURN TO YOUR NEIGHBOR AND SHOUT "THAT'S COPYRIGHTED MATERIAL! THAT'S COPYRIGHTED MATERIAL! I'LL SUE!"

DEEP WOODS OFF **A GUIDE FOR THE UNPREPARED URBAN DWELLER**

You may wear the canvas wear, carry the Sog Paratool and drive the Pathfinder, Explorer or Wagoneer. You may combine them all and drive the Eddie Bauer Northface Ford Explorer. But according to our sources, accouterments a woodsperson does not make. How are you going to save your urban pride and get the most out of your camp experience? Here are some tips from northerners in the know:

WHAT TO EAT:

Enjoy empty calories and nutrient-free nostalgia with a pre-camp feast to pump you up (and out):

- Rubbery chicken. Four out of five dentists recommend it for their patients who chew gum. Doubles as a sight gag at talent show time.
- Dinty Moore. Sure it smells like dog food. But it's stick-to-your-ribs eatin' in a flip-top can.
- Hot dogs and/or beenie weenies. Need we say more?
- French's mustard. A day-glo garnish that's far smoother than Grey Poupon.
- WonderBread. Foccacia has nothing on this vitamin-enriched manna. Bonus: doubles as a sponge at clean-up time. Why else would your mom have bought it?

WHAT TO WEAR:

If you seek the admiration of fellow campers:

- Timberland workboots, Eddie Bauer flannel, CK thermal underwear, stylish canvas "fishing jacket", leather workgloves and an outback hat.

If you seek the disdain of purists:

- See above.

If you seek survival:

- Anything warm. That includes long underwear, sweaters, light gloves and a jacket. October may be colder than you think.

WHAT TO DO:

- Mingle. It's a great place for students to meet mentors or future job contacts. Network for prospective job opportunities, find good advice or a new perspective on business or design issues. It's also a good place to have fun and meet friends. So get out there and do it.
- Dance and, if you wish, drink. Despite the long-standing rumor of the deer antler/Cabin 4/party ball debacle, Design Camp is still a great place to let loose and have fun.
- Learn. Don't skip out on every seminar to forage the area for hidden moose, folk artists or make-out spots. Attend. Learn. Enjoy.
- Play. We're designers. That means we all know what it feels like to be the last one picked in gym class. Rest assured that everyone will play softball, volleyball, or any other ball as poorly as you do—no excuses for not joining in.
- Re-energize. Sometimes the day-to-day grind crushes your creativity. Take this time to regroup and get excited about design again.

WHAT TO WATCH OUT FOR:

- Fire. Keep those synthetic fabrics away from the heat, and everything should go just fine. Look deeply into the flames. If you see Jim Morrison, throw yourself on the fire and scream, "I am the Lizard King."
- Poison Ivy. The three-leaved plant, the oil, the itching, the swelling, the burning. You're going to need an ocean. Of Calamine lotion.
- Skinny Dipping. Oh sure, it sounds great now, but those October waters can send some nasty shivers right down to ye olde timbers. If you must, go in a group. You'll be easier for the rescue team to spot from the helicopter.
- Excessive imbibition. Pace yourself. Keep a copy of *Ladies' Home Journal* on hand at all times. When it starts to look like *Raygun*, call it a night.
- Canoe Tips. But only if you stand up.
- Snakes. Not the clients who stiff you, the reptilian ones that bite. Wear boots, watch where you walk and all will be well. Mind the plumbing, too.

WHAT TO WATCH:

Get in the Design Camp mood with these lovely video choices from the 99-cent rack.

- *Meatballs* Bill Murray before *Ghostbusters*, and a dweeb named Spaz.
- *Deliverance* Ned Beatty in his most penetrating role.
- *Little Darlings* See Tatum O'Neill before John McEnroe.
- *Friday the 13th* Parts I through XIII should keep you occupied well into 1995.
- *Never Cry Wolf* Note the mice-a-roni recipe in case of northwoods mishap.
- *Alive* Tastes like chicken!

DESIGNER S'MORES When you're sitting around that smoky, heartwarming campfire, probing the constellations for inspiration on an annual report design, carbo up with this s'mores recipe—concocted especially for designers.

DESIGNER S'MORES

☐ 1. Lay out graham crackers on high-grade paper towel, preferably on a flat surface (ground is unacceptable). Have a fellow designer get on all fours to provide an appropriate work surface, if necessary.
☐ 2. Cut graham crackers into 2.5" x 2.5" squares. DO NOT BREAK CRACKERS. Use a pre-moistened cotton swab to dampen the perforation line on each individual cracker, then cut with an X-Acto.
☐ 3. Lay out squares of graham cracker in paired units, spaced evenly across the paper towel. Do not overlap.
☐ 4. Unwrap chocolate bar. Hershey's will do, although imported Toblerone or Godiva is preferable. Set aside the wrapping to catch chocolate drippings later.
☐ 5. Cut chocolate bar into 1.3" x 1.3" squares. Locate teflon-coated saucepan. If no saucepan is available, call it a night.
☐ 6. Heat fire to approximately 478° F. Melt chocolate.
☐ 7. While melting chocolate, insert 1/8" sharpened wooden dowels into marshmallows. Roast.
☐ 8. Prepare crackers to receive marshmallows. Once the toasted mallow has been placed on the cracker, allow 5.4 seconds of cooling time before adding 1 teaspoon of chocolate. Complete sandwich with second cracker.
☐ 9. Eat. Enjoy. Make merry. Tell your fellow designer s/he can stop being a table now.

BOARD HIGHLIGHTS

August 2, 1994 6:45 p.m.

Board Present: Barry McCool, Charlie Quimby, Sue Crolick, Allan Haag, Jane Jenni, Karen McCall-Pengra, Steve Wiedorf, Grant Pound, Bruce Rubin, Larry Skov, Dan Woychick, Rory Sparks, Sharon Werner
Guests Present: Gretchen Kuzma, Lynn Tanaka, Geri Thompson and Andy Powell
August Minutes: Werner. Minutes accepted.
Treasurer's Report: Wiedorf (Quimby). No report this month.
Announcements: Pound. AIGA Business Conference is September 24-25 in New York.

Design Camp: Thompson and Powell. The theme of 1994 camp is "Nature of Design, Design of Nature." Main speakers confirmed. Teaser August 1, registration mailed August 17. Camp chairs will investigate moving camp dates for 1995 to the last weekend in September.

Initiatives: McCool. Board reviewed the existing initiatives as proposed by the National AIGA. They were designed to help AIGA focus clearly on its goals and to make it easier for liaisons to get involved in relevant areas. The initiatives and liaisons are: Design History (Volean Pitner), Education (Jo Davison Strand), Environmental Responsibility (Paul Wharton), Internationalism (Lawrence Sanulka), New Technology (Jim Morgan), Professional Issues (no liaison), Public Service (Sue Crolick), Equal Opportunity (no liaison), Business Issues (newly developed). Board will discuss priorities further in the future.

Director Reports:

Exhibitions: Skov. A new directorship for AIGA/Minnesota. Responsible for functions involving the permanent or temporary display of materials and/or information. Goals are to promote AIGA/Minnesota locally and nationally, promote graphic design excellence, provide a vehicle to display work and provide a source of information and inspiration to members. Committee will be formed to initiate priorities set up by Skov.

Remaining reports will be delivered at September meeting.

Priorities: A list of concerns was developed regarding AIGA's strengths, weakness and priorities. These will be reviewed at the September meeting.

Adjourn: 9:36 p.m.

NEWS OF THE WIRED

Norton Utilities 3.0 has been released. Symantec Corp. has upgraded my favorite utilities program for computer repairs. You don't need to understand the problem for Norton to fix it. Run it occasionally to keep yourself out of trouble. And definitely run it if your computer isn't acting right. Norton will also recover your hard drive after a crash. If you don't own Norton Utilities yet, now's a great time to buy it. (P.S. Symantec hasn't paid me a thing to say all of this).

Another software update. Adobe Inc. has come out with Acrobat, an application that lets you send your client a copy of any document that they can view, print and notate, but not alter or edit. They don't need the document application, just a copy of Acrobat. This may not be appropriate for every client, but it may be very helpful for those more design- and computer-savvy clients. I'd sure like to know if anyone is using it, and what their experiences have been...Call me at 375-0077.

MERRI FROMM, LITTLE & CO.

AIGA MIDWEST

client

AMERICAN INSTITUTE
OF GRAPHIC
ARTS/WICHITA

business

GRAPHIC ARTS
ASSOCIATION

design firm

GRETEMAN GROUP

art director

SONIA GRETEMAN

designer

JAMES STRANGE

Like most of this organization's periodicals, this
newsletter shows how well
designers design for other
designers.

pages 12, frequency Special
Issue, quantity 2,000, software QuarkXPress

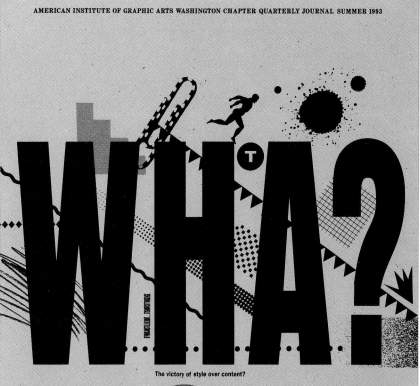

The victory of style over content?

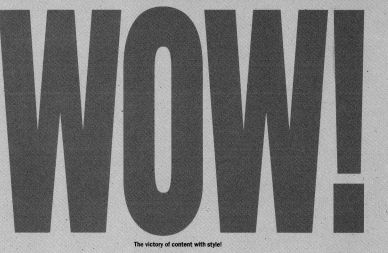

The victory of content with style!

AIGA WASHINGTON CHAPTER QUARTERLY JOURNAL

client

AMERICAN INSTITUTE OF GRAPHIC ARTS/WASHINGTON CHAPTER

business

GRAPHIC ARTS ASSOCIATION

design firm

PAT TAYLOR, INC.

designers

PAT TAYLOR
MARILYN WORSELDINE

Every year AIGA/Washington radically alters its format for the sake of variety and creativity. This larger format printed on a variety of colored paper stocks is a veritable carnival of graphic design.

pages 12, frequency Quarterly, quantity 900, typography Photographic Typesetting

AIGA WASHINGTON
CHAPTER
QUARTERLY
JOURNAL

client

AMERICAN INSTITUTE
OF GRAPHIC
ARTS/WASHINGTON
CHAPTER

business

GRAPHIC ARTS
ASSOCIATION

design firm

PAT TAYLOR, INC.

designer

PAT TAYLOR

illustrators

OPPOSITE
JEFF DEVER
(top left)

PHIL JORDAN
(top right)

TOM SUZUKI
(bottom left)

JULIAN WATERS
(bottom right)

photographer

LARRY CHAPMAN *(left)*

This newsletter is designed
like a small catalog intended
to fit snugly into a standard
envelope. Although its content is limited by its size
and format, it informs and
entertains readers.

pages 24, frequency
Quarterly, quantity 900,
software Pixel Paint, Adobe
Illustrator

ADC
client
**THE ART DIRECTORS
CLUB, INC.**

business
**ART DIRECTORS
ASSOCIATION**

design firm
PENTAGRAM DESIGN

designers
**PAULA SCHER
RON LOUIE**

The newsletter in a magazine format has become a common conceit. This version has a variety of short feature stories, each designed differently to add to the editorial pacing. Two colors are skillfully used to enhance the visual excitement and add another graphic dimension.

pages 24, frequency Quarterly, quantity 5,000

M.Y. How does one enter the graphic arts profession in Poland? **A.D.** Well, after high school, students can apply to the major art academies in the bigger towns like Warsaw or attend a local art college. It takes about six years to complete college in Eastern Europe. They give you a very thorough education, and you have to take many academic subjects. After you graduate, you are automatically accepted into the Artists Guild and get work. If you didn't attend an art academy, you can show your work to the Guild and they'll accept or reject you based on the merit of your work. **M.Y.** Do you feel you've gotten a good art education? **A.D.** Yes. I was very eager to learn. It was a part of my routine to go to the library and do research, something a lot of American students don't like to do. Basically, I spent a lot of time trying to find out what was going on in the West. I wanted to know what was happening in this supposingly better world. I read all the art magazines, like *Graphis* and *Print*. But many of my students here have never even heard of *Graphis*. I suppose if you feel you're living in a better world, you don't care so much about places that don't have it all, unless you're a very socially conscious person. **M.Y.** What kind of resources did they have for artists? **A.D.** We had access to all kinds of foreign magazines. When the system works, the state takes very good care of its citizens. We had free education and free medical services. There was a network of International Press Clubs that operated like coffee bars, and you could go in and read all kinds of publications that were on display. **M.Y.** And when the system wasn't working? **A.D.** You get things like censorship. I got my first dose of it when I was a child. I was reading this French comic book and pages were ripped out of it. The Soviet political system also caused the economic crisis. People didn't work hard because they didn't have to. They couldn't be fired. There was a saying when I was growing up, and it rhymes—it goes, "whether you stand up or you lay down, you still get your minimum wage." And I grew up with this rhyme in the back of my head. People grew up feeling they didn't have to work hard for anything, because it wasn't yours, it was theirs—the Soviets. One of the things that was sanctioned ethically in this very religious country, was stealing from the government. People took tires, typewriters, nuts and bolts and sold them on the black market. This is not only done in Poland but across Eastern Europe. People didn't feel like they were committing a crime because they were resentful of the government. In Poland, it started with five years of very cruel German occupation. During those years people were stealing from the Germans and it was seen as an act of sabotage. This same tactic was used toward the new government, which was officially Polish, but was under the grip of Soviet domination. The

system got more and more corrupt over a period of time. There was no incentive to produce quality products because of the shortages. Anything you put on the store shelves would be gone the next day. When I first came to this country, I had a very hard time explaining to my friends, especially the liberal ones, why Reagan was such a popular figure in Poland. They don't understand it wasn't Reagan himself, but the symbol he represented. He was the one who coined that phrase, "The Evil Empire." This phrase was very much resented in this country, but in Poland, that was how people felt about the Soviet Union. **M.Y.** When you were in Poland, did you have a realistic view of the West? **A.D.** No, not really. I had a glamorized vision of the West. It was hard for me to envision all the defects of the system, like drug addiction and homelessness. For example, if someone was sleeping on the street in Poland, that person would be immediately surrounded by passersby, all wanting to know what happened. **M.Y.** I thought American problems were very well publicized in Communist Block countries. **A.D.** Oh yes. The media was very quick to report on any thing bad that had happened in the U.S., like discrimination of Blacks or crimes in New York. They were front page news. But we didn't believe them. We thought all those stories were exaggerated. Of course, the irony is those were all true stories, but they were used as propaganda, and people got immune to it over time. **M.Y.** Were you considered a dissident artist? **A.D.** Well, I wasn't considered a dangerous figure. The dangerous ones were the writers, journalists and politicians. I did a lot of humorist, satirical cartoons and that made me a household name. Eastern Europe has a long tradition of satirical cartoons. As long as you don't criticize the government directly, or put down the army and the police, you can get away with a lot. Years of political oppression trained artists and writers to work with metaphors and symbols. For example, instead of using human characters, you used animals and insects. Instead of attacking the system directly, you make fun of lazy waiters and corrupt managers. But there is a lack of creative freedom in America, too. **M.Y.** Can you elaborate on this? **A.D.** I see a certain similarity between the communist system and the capitalist system. In Poland, you had to worry about the government; in America you have to worry about the client. The business community puts a lot of pressure on the artists. **M.Y.** In Poland, didn't you have to deal with the person who gave you the assignment? **A.D.** Yes, but the client is usually one person. For example, if I was hired to do a theater poster, my client would be either the director or the theater manager. He'd tell me what the play is about, and

ADC

client

THE ART DIRECTORS
CLUB, INC.

business

ART DIRECTORS
ASSOCIATION

design firm

RE: DESIGN

art director

SEYMOUR CHWAST

A long and narrow size dis-
tinguishes this newsletter
from the average. Yet
because it is printed in black
and white, it is nevertheless
a rather economical format.
When folded, the distinctive
logo and lead story on the
front stand out.

pages 8, frequency
Quarterly, quantity 15,000,
software QuarkXPress

ADC

THE NEWSLETTER
OF THE ART DIRECTORS
CLUB, INC.
FOR ADVERTISING,
GRAPHIC
AND PUBLICATION
DESIGNERS
FALL 1994

LOiS on LOiS

George Lois began his career at 19 as a graphic designer at CBS television. He soon went to Doyle Dane Bernbach where his work included the original Volkswagen campaign. In 1960 he started Papert, Koenig, Lois at a time when art director's names rarely appeared on the front door. Seven years later he set up Lois Holland Callaway, and in 1977 he was named president of Creamer Lois. The following year he became the youngest art director to be inducted into the ADC Hall of Fame. Today Lois is CEO of Lois/USA. He is also recognized for his award-winning Esquire magazine covers. As part of the School of Visual Arts "Master Series," a retrospective exhibition of Lois' work was on view this fall.

The Big Idea

The Big Idea is something you look at that immediately knocks you down. The Big Idea is so fresh, so mind-boggling that it takes a few seconds to realize how terrific an idea it is. It opens your eyes to a product and has a cause and effect when you run the advertising—the next day people go out and buy it. It is also a concept that quickly enters popular language, like: "When you got it, flaunt it," (Braniff Airlines) "I want my MTV," (MTV) and, "Mainframe power in a pizza box," (Data General). All my professional life I only cared about coming up with copy and visuals that would enter the visual culture and literally change the way we look at ourselves.

Paul Rand

Paul Rand changed the world. When you saw one of his ads, you might not say there was a gigantic idea, but it was involving. It had wit. It had surprise. But Rand, great as he was, was too much of an artist. He was a touch embarrassed by selling which is why he endured corporate design. An art director has got to be commercial to a point where he has no regrets. What Rand did for me, and anybody in the '50s and '60s, was inspire us to understand what an art director could bring to graphics. He showed the advertising business that an art director was more than a layout man—he was a conceptual being.

Bill Bernbach

Advertising changed when Bill Bernbach entered the business. Bill was a very fine writer, but he also put together the first conceptual advertising team that married the talent of a great art director, designer and writer—it was an epiphany. Bernbach also knew how to put together a concept and the right atmosphere to make it happen. He got the best out of people. When I went to work for Doyle Dane Bernbach, I was called a maverick because I brought a street sense. For Kerid ear wax, I did a gigantic ear with pencils and paper clips sticking out of it and everybody was shocked. Bill, however, recognized that I did advertising that locked you in, set you back. He elevated the art director to an equal level with the writer. For him, the art director was a genius and he invested the position with power.

Marketing vs. Design

I do not accept people's marketing strategies. I listen, but almost always the strategy and the positioning are unambitious. Any great creative person listens to those around him, to marketing strategies, gathers all the research possible, and then comes up with an answer that goes beyond anything that anybody had thought of. That is what is wrong with agencies these days. The marketing people come up with a strategy that they then present to the creative people by saying, "Here, fulfill this." The creative team is then handcuffed and in most cases the work is restricted. One of the biggest problems with advertising is not that it is not talented but it's wrong-headed, and the wrong-headness often comes from traditional marketing people.

The Surprise

The surprise is the execution of a strategy that changes, broadens, pinpoints, does something with it that is startlingly different. The idea I put down must always be surprising, one that shakes up a lot of people in the agency and at the client. When I did Data General and saw that they had a new product, I came up with "Mainframe Power in a Pizza Box." The brains of a small computer were roughly that size. When I gave them the tag line, I was saying that the image of the company is going to be a pizza box. Naturally, all these techies cried, "Our symbol is a pizza box?" The idea of taking a complicated machine that even the CEO does not entirely understand and say in a humanistic way that all this power which once took up three rooms is now a pizza box is startling. The campaign, however, was enormously successful, business tripled and the stock shot up 2 to 26. But you have to fight for that kind of idea because people are so willing to kill it. Our job is not only to create good ideas, but to fight for them.

The Watchdog Copier

The first ad campaign for a Minolta copier is about to be launched. In the literature about the machine they say that the copier has three hidden electronic watchdogs. I saw the word "watchdog" and immediately thought, "What a great campaign! I will call it the Watchdog copier and use a German shepherd as the symbol." The commercial starts with "Only from the minds of Minolta." It fades to black and then comes this German shepherd that growls. What defines Minolta is only this dog, the watchdog. Meanwhile, people are making copies: a young man makes copies, says, "Good watchdog" and pats the dog; a woman makes copies and says, "Nice watchdog," the owner of the company says, "Smart watchdog," etc. It took Minolta some time to realize that this would be the first copier with a personality. Very few people in American business know that Minolta makes copiers. Now they'll all say, "What about that watchdog thing?" Suddenly, from nobody looking at you, 100% of the business is looking at you! The important thing is to come up with an idea that seems outrageous but in actual fact isn't.

Power

When I left Doyle Dane Bernbach, I started Papert, Koenig, Lois. Now my name was on the front door which added more power to the art direc-

CONTINUED ON PAGE 4

The Passion of Mohammed Ali photographed by Carl Fischer for the April 1968 cover of *Esquire* magazine.

THE ART DIRECTORS CLUB, INC.
250 PARK AVENUE SOUTH
NEW YORK, NY 10003

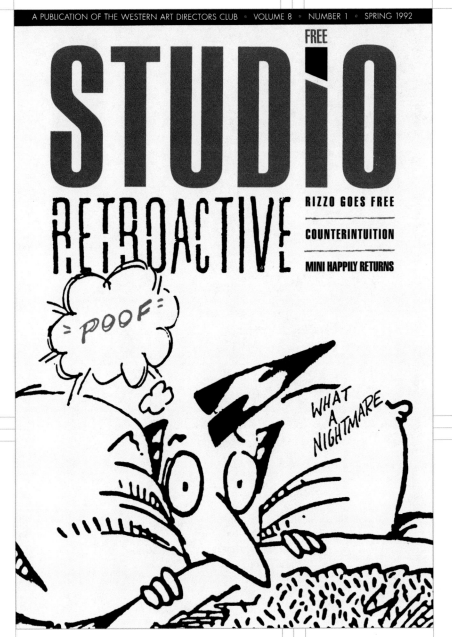

STUDIO

client
**WESTERN ART
DIRECTORS CLUB**

business
**ART DIRECTORS
ASSOCIATION**

design firms
THARP DID IT

HALLECK DESIGN
(masthead)

designers
**JANA HEER
JOE MILLER
JEAN MOGANNAM
RICK THARP**

illustrator
JOE MURRAY

The blown-up line illustration on the cover of this newspaper-sized publication gives a sense of immediacy. The bold type demands that the reader take notice.

pages 10, frequency Quarterly, software QuarkXPress

(DIGITAL DESIGNERS GROUP)
6466 FAIRCREST ROAD
COLUMBUS, OHIO 43229

**If you see a tree as blue,
then make it blue.** PAUL GAUGUIN

PERSONALITY

HEREDITY

EXPERIENCE

SEX

CULTURE

light + objects + eye/brain + psychological factors = color perception

D2G NEWSLETTER

client

D2G DIGITAL DESIGNERS GROUP

business

CLUB OF MACINTOSH DESIGNERS

design firm

SCHMELTZ + WARREN

art director/ designer

CRIT WARREN

photographer

CRIT WARREN

This folded broadsheet newsletter opens up into a billboard of information layered with type and images. Its form is well suited to the job of getting news out immediately.

pages Foldout, frequency Monthly, quantity 500, software Macintosh

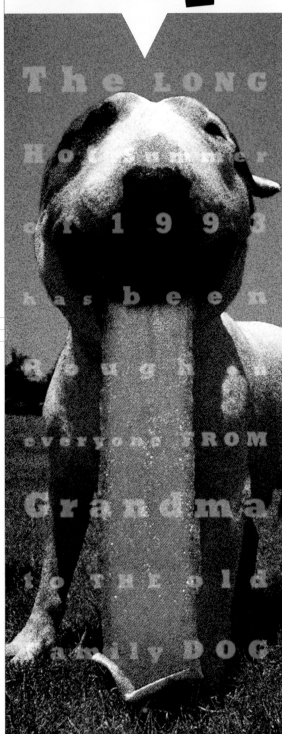

A Publication of the Dallas Society of Visual Communications — August 1993, Volume Three, Issue Number One, Five Dollars

ROUGH

ROUGH
client

DALLAS SOCIETY OF VISUAL COMMUNICATIONS
business

VISUAL COMMUNICATIONS
design firm

BRAINSTORM, INC.
art directors/ designers

CHUCK JOHNSON
KEN KOESTER
ROB SMITH

illustrators

JACK UNRUH
KEN KOESTER
CHUCK JOHNSON
ROB SMITH
AND OTHERS

photographers

PHIL HOLLENBECK
AND OTHERS

The logo or masthead is about the only thing that remains constant in this crazy collection of publications. Size, shape, format—everything—is up for grabs in this conspicuous display of graphic exuberance. Continued on pages 30 and 31.

pages Varies, frequency Monthly, quantity 1,500, software QuarkXPress, Adobe Illustrator, Adobe Photoshop

The LONG Hot Summer of 1993 has been dough to everyone FROM Grandma' to the old family DOG

LONG HOT SUMMER

It's hot outside. Really hot. Suffocating hot. Texas hot. The kind of hot that hits you like a boxing glove and wraps around you like a leaden overcoat. Day after day of molasses-syrup-gnat-infested air. Is this what they call the Dog Days of Summer? If so, I'm not sure why. My dogs won't even venture out into this planetary oven. Instead, they stand statue-like at the windows, gazing at the squirrels busily performing a search-and-destroy mission on our bird feeders. Reminiscing, no doubt, about crisp autumn days when nothing but a flapping Johnson Door stood between them and full-speed rodent annihilation. After a few minutes of this silent introspection, doggie sighs echo throughout the house and they head for the coldest expanse of floor tile they can find. Hey. Maybe that's what this Dog Day thing is really all about. As deadlines loom, nothing in my world is moving. Not a leaf. Not the air. Certainly not my fingers on the keyboard. I think I'll lie down, press my skin against the cool, smooth surface of our Spanish tile and think about October for awhile.

A Publication of the Dallas Society of Visual Communications · November 1993, Volume Three, Issue Number Three, Five Dollars

ROUGH

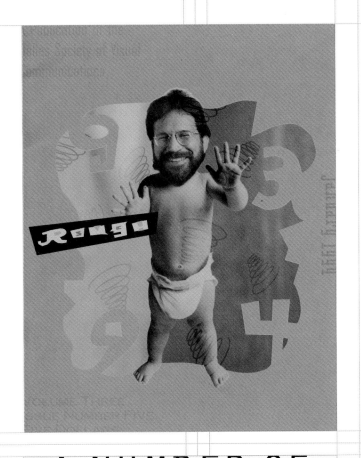

A NUMBER OF
PEOPLE IN
THIS BUSINESS
CAN BE BOUGHT.

ROUGH

A PUBLICATION OF THE DALLAS SOCIETY OF VISUAL COMMUNICATIONS, FEBRUARY 1994, VOLUME THREE, ISSUE NUMBER SIX, FIVE DOLLARS

A QUARTERLY PUBLICATION OF THE SOCIETY FOR ENVIRONMENTAL GRAPHIC DESIGN

Spring 92
Volume 6
Number 1

Message(s)egd

PATHways
TO DESIGN

PATH

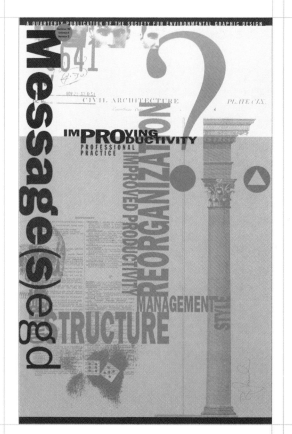

MESSAGES

client

SOCIETY FOR ENVIRONMENTAL GRAPHIC DESIGN

business

GRAPHIC ARTS ASSOCIATION

design firm

STOLTZE DESIGN

designer

CLIFFORD STOLTZE

Three colors are cheaper than four and often just as effective. This newsletter is formatted like a tabloid magazine with display ads and classifieds, also proving that inexpensive newsletters are only a step away from commercial publishing.

pages 24-26, frequency Quarterly, quantity 1,500

MECHANISM

client

COLUMBUS SOCIETY
OF COMMUNICATING
ARTS

business

ORGANIZATION OF
CREATIVE
COMMUNICATING
PROFESSIONALS

creative
director

CRIT WARREN
(overall concept)

designer

CRIT WARREN
(mailing envelope/stickers)

photographer

CRIT WARREN
(mailing stickers)

This is more than just a
new-wave approach; it is a
fine specimen of packaging.
The newsletter comes in a
specially designed envelope
which is sealed with an
illustrated sticker. Inside
the typography and imagery
are decidedly contemporary.
Continued on pages
36 to 39.

pages Foldout, frequency
10/year, quantity 750

CSCA 2142 Wesleyan Drive Columbus Ohio 43221

1.16
MECHANISM

Columbus Society of Communicating Arts

1.16

MECHANISM

creative
director/
designer

CRIT WARREN

art directors

CRIT WARREN
LORI TRENEFF

(opposite)

designers

KIRK DONNAN
ROD JOSLIN

photographer

ROD JOSLIN

this
i
take
or
it

PRESERVATION = SALVATION

Use a reservoir-tip condom, or pinch the end of a condom to create a space for semen. Place a drop of spermicide inside the tip of the condom, for both lubrication and protection. While holding the tip with one hand, put the condom on the head of the erect penis with the other, and slowly and carefully unroll the condom down the shaft of the penis to the base, smoothing out air bubbles. Have a spare available in case you find holes or the condom tears during intercourse. Apply a water-based lubricant to the covered penis, as well as spermicide to your partner. After ejaculation, grip the condom at the base of the penis and withdraw while the penis is still erect. Dispose of the condom, and use a new one each time you have intercourse.

There lingers in the air the possibility of losing what we have. As a people, as an earth, as a universe. More and more, questions are posed, though to no one out loud. What could have been? Who might have been? The scent of new, green corn under a glowing sun. The scent of a love that could be the love that's forever. Though nothing, individually, is just one thing, everything is ultimately connected as one. Taking care of self and what surrounds us is no longer a choice. Rather, it is an ultimatum. (With apologies to Virginia Woolf.)

CSCA 2142 Wesleyan Drive Columbus Ohio 43221

5.21
MECHANISM

art directors/
designers
CRIT WARREN
LORI TRENEFF

(opposite)
designer
PAUL NINI

Columbus Society of Communicating Arts

5.21
MECHANISM

Quick!
What does this strange little appendage have to do with the upcoming CSCA Third Thursday?

– The Mechanism staff is doing a survey of artsy gifts
for under a buck?
– Your membership dues are hard at work?
– Ah, it s Spring, and love is in the air?

Give up?
Page 2!

Words.

The more we use them, the less they mean. Take "graphic design" for instance – just what is it anyway? If you go to your local print shop they may tell you they do graphic design. So will many highly-trained, and in relation, highly paid consultants or corporate designers. Obviously there's a huge difference in the quality of services and finished products between the two extremes cited (or so we hope). Does this situation bother you? It bothers me.

In my opinion the term "graphic design" has lost its significance. It's come to mean too much, and now it means very little. The term was originally conceived by the field's early practitioners as a way to differentiate their activities from those of their counterparts in advertising and commercial art. They saw their practices focusing on the design of informative communications instead of those meant to persuade. Their hope was that "graphic design" would develop into a true problem-solving profession (as opposed to a service profession) with a status akin to that of architecture's.

What differentiates a true profession from a service profession you may ask? A service-oriented business generally offers a number of predetermined products or services to customers or clients. For instance, a barber provides haircuts, shampoos, shaves, etc. A professional-oriented business, however, typically utilizes a "process" for serving clients, and a body of knowledge and theory that is drawn from when conducting that process. A lawyer, though he or she may specialize in one area of the law, must investigate a client's situation, analyze it, look at precedents, and prescribe an appropriate course of action. Investigation, analysis and planning now enter the equation, and there the distinction lies.

Where does "graphic design" fall into this framework? Somewhere in the middle, but closer to the service side I'm afraid. Some graphic designers do conduct investigation and analysis to inform their form-making, but the majority do not. That is why graphic design has never achieved the status of a true profession, and has been historically viewed as the poor step-child of the design fields. How did "graphic design" lose its original intent to become professionally-oriented? Simply put; by focusing on the product (form-making) and not the process.

Form-making is an extremely important part of what we graphic designers do. Please don't misunderstand me, I'm not advocating that form-making become less important. I'm merely suggesting that we make the earlier stages of the design process (investigation, analysis and planning) equally important. These activities should not be left to marketing people, as their primary focus is on finding better ways to sell goods and services. Graphic design is about selling at times, but just as often it's about providing information – and that's something most marketeers know little about. Graphic designers should be involved in analyzing a client's communications, and finding ways to provide information that is of strategic value. Transforming complicated product and pricing information into an easily understood form is one example of a communication that is of strategic benefit to a client, and that would be greatly appreciated by the end-user. Clearly this type of activity requires a focused and well-defined process to solve a particular problem, and problem solving is what true "professionals" do.

Stylistic and form-making developments generally receive the most attention from graphic designers. That is appropriate, as no one would wish to see one style of form-making used in all situations. There are, obviously, many different types of audiences with different concerns and expectations. A style utilized for a communication geared to one audience is probably not valid for a communication geared to another audience. The ability to understand the concerns and expectations of audiences can only be achieved through incorporating investigative and analytical activities prior to the development of form-making. It is graphic design's inability (or refusal) to do this that has resulted in its current less-than-professional stature.

What about the term "visual communication"? Many of us see it merely as a fancy way of saying "graphic design". I define visual communication as the process of providing pictorial and written information to an intended audience. There are, in my opinion, two important distinctions that separate visual communication from graphic design. The first is that visual communication is a "process", that by its problem-solving nature includes investigative and analytical skills in the creation of communications. Graphic design focuses primarily on form-making, while visual communication incorporates a broader series of efforts to provide rationale for form-making. The second distinction is that visual communication includes other types of communications beyond printed matter (graphic design's mainstay). The design of interactive computer presentations that integrate video, animation, sound, stored images and text is also included in this definition (like it or not, this will be a major activity of tomorrow's designers).

Many changes in our roles as designers are in store for this decade and the coming century. There will be significant advances in how we practice and how we educate newcomers to our field. If we wish to progress towards a more substantial professional stature we must incorporate additional concerns and skills into our practice, and provide ways to incorporate these skills into our educational programs. It's clear that to produce a designer that is literate, well-educated and adept at utilizing analytical processes and creating sophisticated form will take more than four years of undergraduate education. Consequently, there will be a new emphasis on graduate design education (one Ph.D. program in design already exists in the US, more will likely be created). On the other hand, the profession may be asked to provide more student work experiences, where critical hands-on and technical training can be most easily supplied.

Our field is being forced to grow up.

If it doesn't it will eventually become irrelevant. Facilitating changes such as those discussed above will be the emphasis of educators like myself. Whether we call ourselves graphic designers or visual communicators is of little importance. The important thing is that we move our field forward. Our future depends on it.

Have a nice day. :·)

This is a picture of my grandfather – he was a barber. Now you know why I've chosen this example.

Investigation

| Recognize a Need |

| Identify the Problem |

Analysis/Planning

| Gather Information |

| Analyze Information |

| Develop a Plan |

Synthesis/Evaluation

| Design Prototypes |

| Evaluate Prototypes |

| Produce a Solution |

| Evaluate Responses |

Steps that can make-up a typical design process. Highlighted steps are those usually ignored by graphic designers, but that are critical to any professional practice.

Rhode Island School of Design already offers a five year "Bachelor of Graphic Design" degree for those who wish to go beyond the typical Bachelor of Fine Arts.

The Institute of Design at IIT in Chicago has recently created the first Ph.D. in Design program in the United States.

Look! Even Sir Speedy is a graphic designer!

Cinderella with a T-square: graphic design as the poor step-child.

Graphic Design or Visual Communication: Product vs. Process

by Paul Nini

Paul Nini is an Assistant Professor of Visual Communication at the Department of Industrial Design, the Ohio State University. He would like to thank the CSCA for this opportunity to voice his opinions.

art directors

CRIT WARREN
LORI TRENEFF

designers

CRIT WARREN
LORI TRENEFF
GREG BONNELL-KANGAS
(Camp CSCA cricket logo)

(opposite)
designer

KIRK RICHARD SMITH

photographer

STEPHEN WEBSTER

HERE. TAKE THIS LITTLE QUIZ:

PORTION OF YOUR SERVICES SHOULD YOU BE CHARGING SALES TAX?

"GETTING PAID," WHAT DOES IT MEAN WHEN YOU ENDORSE A CHECK?

ACCEPTING A MONEY ORDER PROTECT YOU?

MECHANISM

8.20

Columbus Society of Communicating Arts

street Dreams

\# 1

ARTSWORD

client

PENN STATE SCHOOL OF VISUAL ARTS

business

UNIVERSITY

design firm

SOMMESE DESIGN

art director

KRISTIN SOMMESE

designers/ photographers

KRISTIN SOMMESE JIM LILLY

ARTSWORD

volume **1**, number **1**, Fall 1993

Dear Friends & Alums,

I hope you will enjoy this, our first ever School of Visual Arts newsletter. It is long overdue and we have a lot to catch up on. Plans at present are to get subsequent editions to you annually. **Fourteen years have passed** since the Department of Art Education merged with the Department of Art to form the SVA. During this period there have been many changes in the facilities and programs of the School such more to come over the next several years. **The School of Visual Arts** presently occupies all or parts of several campus buildings. The Visual Arts Building, the School's primary studio/classroom office structure, is located close to the Creamery. It is connected to the Palmer Museum of Art which is undergoing a 5.7 million dollar expansion (pictured above) designed by noted architect, Charles Moore. **The former Crafts Building,** now called the Arts Cottage, is the current home of art education Classroom and studio space remain in portions of Chambers Building and on the second floor of the Arts Building. We are in the process of **renovating the Patterson Building,** one of the older brick "Ag Hill" buildings across from the Museum, for SVA use. Completion of these renovations in the spring of 1994 will mark the end of an era for art education in Chambers. At that time, all remaining studio and classroom there will move to Patterson which will also house a well equipped Macintosh teaching CAD lab and a "high end" College research CAD Lab. **The SVA administrative offices will move** to Patterson as well, creating space for a large, newly needed seminar room in the Visual Arts Building. Although the moves will not increase overall square footage, they will bring the various components of our program physically closer together and make the School's available space more useful. **Over the last decade** enrollment of undergraduate students in our two programs, studio art and art education, has grown tremendously. It is now approaching 300 majors, the largest number in our history. Demand by non-majors for SVA courses is also unprecedented. However, as we continue to struggle to accommodate the youngsters of student interest in the visual arts we are seemingly confident of a bright future. **Many of the School's one senior faculty members,** with whom large numbers of alumni studied, have retired over the past ten years. Although these professors are missed we have been fortunate to recruit a number of able and dedicated newer faculty who are carrying on the School's tradition of excellence. We are taking the opportunity in these pages to acquaint you with some of their activities along with those of faculty whose names may be more familiar. **I want to thank the hundreds of alumni** who answered my brief questionnaire and returned the questionnaire for your reservation response. Your texts and comments brought back many wonderful memories to those of us who reviewed the feedback. I trust that you will understand that the newsletter staff, because of the volume and length of your responses, may have been able to include only small bits and pieces of the information you submitted. However, an effort has been made to distill something about everyone who returned the form, of your many achievements, and on campus in the near future to enter you back to share your memories and accomplishments in more detail. We also plan to work your input in to shape our future. **Sincerely,**

We are very proud

James Stephenson, Director
School of Visual Arts

❶

View of the Palmer Museum of Art.

View of Patterson Building

---

s t u d e n t   n e w s

STUDENT WINS GRAPHIC DESIGN AWARD

A Gold Award for student work was recently awarded to graphic design student Kelly Thompson by **Studio Magazine** in its seventh awards annual issue, 1992/93. Selected for publication by a panel of professional judges, Kelly's photographic design entry was directed by graphic design professor **Kristin Breslin Sommese.** The annual awards program recognizes **international excellence** in graphic design, art direction, illustration, photography, printing and TV commercials and video including student work. The winning pieces are coming Canada and the United States. **Congratulations Kelly**

❹

MURAL PROJECT CONTINUES PENN STATE TRADITION

Five multicultural murals, created by University students, faculty and staff under the direction of **Sarita Barrows,** assistant professor of art, were exhibited at the University's Hetzel Union Building Browsing Gallery in January and February. The murals, each measuring 8 x 11 feet, represent the cultural diversity of Penn State. They depict **Native Americans, Latino Americans/Hispanics, African Americans and other groups** which combine to provide the rich and varied cultural heritage of the University's resident populations. After their exhibition in the gallery, the murals were displayed in residence hall lounges. **According to Ann Shields,** assistant director of the HUB art galleries, the mural project brought together students, faculty and staff from the Office of Student Affairs and the School of Visual Arts in a collaborative effort. **Prior to the actual painting** of the murals, students met with various groups and associations on campus including The Black Caucus, the Puerto Rican Student Association, the Latino Caucus, the Asian American Student Coalition, the Native American Indian Student Association and the University Student Advisory Board in order to gather ideas for the imagery contained in the works. The mural painting tradition according to Barrows, has an ancient history on the American continent. In the 20th century. We save artist used the mural to foster that country's nationalism. The mural movement flowered in the United States in the 1930s and '40s, partly as a consequence of the great depression and federal support for visual artists. In recent decades the mural movement has been continued by universities as well as social and political activist artist. **What many may not realize is that** the project represents the continuation of a rich mural tradition at Penn State carried on by University art and art education faculty and students since the 1940s. This tradition produced murals painted in Old Main in 1940-1949 by Henry Varnum Poor assisted by then senior art student Stuart Frost, murals by Penn State student John Biggers in Barrows Building and the Paul Robeson Cultural Center, murals by George Pappas and other former Penn State students located, and recently, in Chambers Building, and murals by former students George Zoretich and Bryan Williams in the Mineral Industries Building. **Many examples of these wonderful murals,** a number of those remaining social, political, and multicultural content, found their way into Penn State buildings as a result of the murals course developed and taught by Viktor Lowenfeld and continued after Lowenfeld's death by Joe Chomicki. Large scale works by student from Chomicki's classes continue to grace the walls of buildings on Calder Alley and may be found at other locations in the State College community. Professor Barrows ably carries on the tradition in these more recent artistic celebrations of diversity. One of the murals will be reproduced as a poster and for Penn State.

---

❺

Sallie McCorkle and Thomas McGovern have spent the past year overseeing the development of their joint creation **The Barn Raising, a large commissioned outdoor public sculpture** for the Milton S. Hershey Medical Center in Hershey, Pa. The idea developed as a response to the farmlands which surround the center. The **artists wished to create a piece** that served as a tribute to the region's cultural heritage and to all individuals who gather together to make manifest monumental ideas. The sculpture sits on a grassy knoll in front of the entrance to the University and Children's hospital. **It is a sealed-down replica** of a standard barn structure with the back wall fixed in a tilted position as it in the process of being raised. Outside the barn is a table made to look like wooden planks on sawhorses. Next to the table is a bench that resembles a plank on produce crates. The entire structure is **made of steel and painted red.** It is an esthetic sculpture may enter the barn or sit at the table. An identification sign, which normally accompanies a work of art, is incorporated into the sculpture. On top of the table, an engraved plaque replicates an architect's drawing of the barn's structure and contains the title and dedication information. McCorkle and McGovern have involved their students in the project. As a result, **these students have gained a better understanding of the complex activities that are a necessary part of any public art commission.** Their discussions have addressed the development of proposals and models, interactions with structural engineers, safety and budget issues, and the final fabrication and installation.

---

by Jim Lilly

The spring of 1993 saw the coming and going of another **Undergraduate Exhibition.** The exhibit, which opened on March 11th at the Zoller Gallery 101 Visual Arts Bldg, included **102 works by 82 artists.** A total of 399 works by 143 artists was submitted to be practically sculpted into a cohesive show by this year's juror **John Vanco,** Director of the Erie Art **Museum,** Erie, PA. Director Vanco's candor and experience can be appreciated through his jurors statements written for the events catalog. He stated "I was able relatively rapidly to select a large number of works and then slowly chip away to reveal an exhibition which reflects the strengths of this department (and disabilities to) some extent my own tastes and predjudices." With that he went on to pick the shows prize winners **Robert Lynch** for his piece "Malcolm X II", **Malcolm Mobuto** for his work "Umbrage", and **Susan Conard** for her piece "A Day at the Zoo". Honorable mentions went to Cara Joshua Altishell, Bill Hosserman, and Brian Brosh Craig. To all the artists whose works were accepted into the show, **congratulations.** To those artists who did not get into the show, I quote, "Not putting one on display, they shine forth. Not justifying themselves, they are distinguished. Not boasting, they receive recognition. Not bragging, they never falter. They do not quarrel, so no one quarrels with them. The refuse the ancients say **'Yield and overcome.'** Is that an empty saying? Be really whole. And all things will come to you." *Jim Lilly is a graduating senior in Graphic Design*

DID YOU KNOW?

client
PENN STATE SCHOOL
OF VISUAL ARTS

business
UNIVERSITY

design firm
PENN STATE DESIGN
PRACTICOMM

art director
LANNY SOMMESE

designers/
photographers
COLLEEN MEADE
COLLEEN TOOHEY

This long and narrow, one-
color publication is graphically very bold. However,
the use of a light-line typeface for the text makes this
as difficult to read as it is
enjoyable to view.

pages 8, frequency
Biannually, quantity 1,000,
software QuarkXPress

did y?u kn?w?

MARCH 1994

A NEWSLETTER FOR THOSE WHO WANT TO STAY IN THE KNOW

W e l c o m e !

The School of Visual Arts faculty and staff welcome you to our new office in Patterson Building. The SVA office, located in room 210, will be open Monday through Friday 8 am-noon and 1-5pm. Along with the change of location, we are creating a more accessible resource center for you, to find information relating to you chosen profession of art. This first attempt will extend to you the opportunity to receive up-to-date information relating to the field of art. We will be printing a newsletter entitled, DID YOU KNOW? which will carry vital information concerning the arts. DID YOU KNOW? will inform SVA students about various local, regional, national, and international opportunities. This newsletter will feature students sharing their trials, tribulations, hard work and person-al achievements in the world of art. For these students this information has become an invalu-able tool, but for you it can become a well spring of experiences from which you can draw from your future endeavors. Copies of DID YOU KNOW? will be available in Patterson building in the second floor lobby. Students who are interested in contributing informa-tion for print contact Dori Lemeh in room 210 Patterson Building.

OPPORTUNITIES

What, summer already! Well, "The early bird catches the worm" does apply to the student who looks ahead and is prepared for all opportunities that Penn State has to offer. The following are just a few activities which can be both advantageous and rewarding

SUMMER STUDY
TRAVEL ABROAD

Gain Penn State credit, travel overseas, visit museums throughout Europe, enhance your education. Take advantage of a wonderful opportunity which the School of Visual Arts has organized for the artist of the future — the Study Abroad Program in Todi, Italy. Each summer a faculty member from the College of Arts & Architecture serves as a mentor, guide, teacher, and adviser to a group of students who wish to try their wings abroad in Italy. Last year, Jean Sanders, assistant professor in printmaking, served as the organizer for the program. This year John Kissick, associate professor in painting and drawing, will host the students for this event. If you are interested in learning more about Penn State's Education Abroad programs, contact **Education Abroad Programs** Penn State University 222 Boucke Building 865-7681 FAX: 865-3336. There are a few awards based upon need available to the student who is interested in traveling abroad, but is financially unable to do so. Contact Sherry Walk in the international office. Education Abroad 865-7681

AN INTERVEIW WITH BFA SCULPTURE STUDENT
GATHONI KAMAU AND
MFA PRINTMAKER
BILL MEISBURGER

Gathoni, why did you decide to travel abroad to Todi, Italy? I initially considered both Todi, Italy, and Puebla, Mexico. Each place historically and artistically appealed to me as an artist. I was in need of a change. I was feeling stagnant, so I began searching for an outlet for further artistic growth. Both programs offered me an opportunity for growth. **Bill, after learning about the program, what steps did you take in order to qualify for the Todi program?** I attended an informal meeting scheduled by the Education Abroad Program. After viewing slides and talking with students who had previously attended the program, I filled out an application. The application procedure included a brief essay, letters of recommendation, and an interview by a committee. The committee consisted of the director of the Education Abroad Program and the instructor for the Todi program, Kristi Wormhoudt headed the interview process. **Gathoni, what about living arrangements?** We lived and ate with Italian families in Todi, which gave us a sense of belonging to the community. I do not speak Italian, and sometimes communication was difficult, but I managed. **So you are not required to speak Italian before going to Todi?** No. I had never studied Italian prior to the Todi program. There is no language prerequisite for applying to the program. However, we had daily lessons in Italian to enable us to communicate with our host families. It is easier to speak the language of a country when you hear the language spoken by the people native to the region. **Bill, What about travel arrangements for the students?** Our airline tickets and living arrangements were made by Kristi Wormhoudt, the head of the Todi Program. The program is highly efficient and the travel arrangements went smoothly. Students interested in making their own travel arrangements were allowed to. **Gathoni and Bill, did your trip abroad influence you artistically?** To some degree I was influenced artistically. As a craftsperson, I am interested in similarities in the pattern designs on the clay pots and some African cultural designs. I found the designs on the pots in Italy very delicate and beautiful. (Bill) While I was in Italy, I wanted to try my hand at watercoloring. The whole countryside lent itself to my broadening my artistic scope through the watercolor medium. By traveling to different museums, anthropological sites, and other places such as Venice and Pompeii, I couldn't help but be influenced by the historic artistry of my surroundings. **Did either of you have the opportunity to visit other towns or cities?** (Gathoni) Well, we were all given the opportunity to travel to different cities and villages. Students traveled by bus, car, train, and boat. On our visit to Pompeii, we saw how the lava preserved the Pompeian people either outside running or inside sleeping. When we visited Venice, we went by boat through the canals of the city. It was an experience I will always remember. (Bill) We visited 18 cities, always returning to Todi for study. We went to Rome, Venice, Pompeii, and Assisi, and on my own I traveled to Verona during our four day break. We discovered the charms of the smaller towns such as Orvieto, Spoleto, Tarquinia, and Derota. **How would you sum up the whole Todi experience, and what advice would you give to your fellow students?** (Gathoni) If you have the opportunity and means to do so, then go. The time we spent there was magnificent. Visiting Venice, Florence, Pompeii an experience that I will always remember. (Bill) I would happily recommend going to Todi, Italy, with Penn State. Once there, I would tell students to open their minds and hearts to the culture of Italy. The rewards are immeasurable. You become a part of two families your host family and your "family" of fellow students. Always carry yourself with dignity, because you serve as an unofficial representative of the United States. This is a two—way dialogue between Americans and Italians. Your fellow students can also become close to you. This is a magical and inspiring journey. Artistically and emotionally, this program will stay with you and help sustain you in everyday life. Finally, I would say to every student "Dare to challenge your preconceived notions of the world and its people." You will unlock doors in Italy that will serve as a passage way to understanding America and your people when you return

SUMMER
INTERNSHIPS

Job experience, college credits and possibly a salary for summer work is a gold mine for you. Interviewers always ask the question, "Do you have the job experience relating to this position?" Be prepared to answer the question with a resounding "Yes!"

AN INTERVIEW WITH BFA PRINTMAKING STUDENT
BILL HOSTERMAN

Bill, how did you first learn about the internship with printmaker Kathy Carracio? Last fall semester the printmaking area organized a bus trip for the students to visit Bob Blackburn's Printmaking Workshop in New York. At the printshop, you have the opportunity to meet regional, national, and international artists. While we were touring Bob Blackburn's facility, Kathy Carracio stopped to talk to the group. Kathy Carracio had worked at Bob Blackburn's Printmaking Workshop for at least 10 years. She teaches at New York University and owns her own print shop. Kathy mentioned that she would help students who were interested in interning with her shop. I took her name and number, then I followed up with a phone call. I visited the print shop on several occasions, meeting other printmakers each time I went to New York. In order to see if we could work together, it became necessary for me to take trips to Kathy's print shop in New York. **When and where did the internship take place?** Last summer in New York. **Who did you consult with, and which course number was used?** I spoke with my printmaking professor, Robin Gibson, concerning the internship with Kathy Carracio. For college credit, I used the Art 496 Independent Study course number. **How were you graded?** Before I left for New York, Robin and I discussed how I was to be graded. She let me know what was to be expected from me. A combination of 40 hours of studio work and a report were the basis of my grade. **What did you hope to accomplish by working in both studios among professional artists?** I wanted and needed to gain practical work experience in a professional workshop. I developed my skills as a printmaker, learned new techniques I can apply to my own work, saw how print-shops make money, and observed how

LANDSCAPE ARCHITECTURE AT PENN STATE

client

PENN STATE DEPT. OF LANDSCAPE ARCHITECTURE

business

UNIVERSITY

design firm

PENN STATE DESIGN PRACTICOMM

art director

LANNY SOMMESE

designers

DARA SCHMINKE CHEMI MONTES

The unique identity of this black and white tabloid rests on its distinctive typography. It is at once a news report and a lasting document.

pages 16, frequency Annually, quantity 5,000, software QuarkXPress

F&V

client

WEXNER CENTER FOR THE ARTS

business

CONTEMPORARY ARTS CENTER

design firm

WEXNER CENTER DESIGN DEPARTMENT

designer

M. CHRISTOPHER JONES

This is another inexpensive web-printed newsletter that exploits "dirty" printing characteristics (i.e., smudged color and gray halftones) to best advantage. Its rough-hewn cast is intentionally immediate, and is a fitting frame for the timely information contained inside.

pages 4, frequency Bimonthly, quantity 7,500, software QuarkXPress, Aldus PageMaker, Adobe Illustrator, Aldus Freehand, Adobe Photoshop

CRANBROOK
ACADEMY OF ART ALUMNI · OUTLINE

SPRING 1994

The **architecture** of Cranbrook continues to be recognized in many ways. The programs and projects of the Architecture Department, headed by Dan Hoffman, will receive recognition in the forthcoming publication *Architecture Studio* by Rizzoli. The buildings of Eliel Saarinen have been praised as a masterwork of American architecture and the restored Saarinen House will bring even further acclaim. Plans for the new studios by Rafael Moneo promise to further this tradition of excellence. The following is extracted from the foreword written by Roy Slade, President of the Academy, for the Rizzoli publication *Architecture Studio*. ✆ *The Architecture Studio at Cranbrook Academy of Art, since its beginning under Eliel Saarinen in 1932, has endeavored to extend the understanding of architecture into broader realms. This imperative comes in part from the Studio's presence in a graduate art academy that has always covered a wide range of artistic and craft-based disciplines, an environment in which each discipline is challenged to work at its limit to find areas of common interest and concern. Saarinen encouraged his students to experiment in the various ways of working found at the Academy. The results can be seen in the highly individualistic work of such former graduates as Fumihiko Maki, Harry Weese, Eero Saarinen, Ralph Rapson, Edmund Bacon, Ray and Charles Eames, Florence Knoll, and Harry Bertoia, whose work reveals profound respect for crafts and knowledge of the processes of artistic production. This interest in the relationship between art and craft may be Saarinen's most enduring influence at the Academy. This interest is also reflected in Cranbrook's buildings and grounds, created by Saarinen and others. Thought not of a particular school or style,they demonstrate an abiding faith that an intimate contact with the processes and materials of artistic production inevitably leads to beautiful and meaningful work. Since I arrived at Cranbrook in 1977, I have noted that the students and members of the Academy are inspired by the possibilities and demands of crafting a work of art or architecture. I*

OUTLINE

client
CRANBROOK ACADEMY OF ART

business
ART INSTITUTE

design firm
CRANBROOK ACADEMY OF ART

designers
ELIZABETH GRYBAUGH DENISE HECKMAN

The diminishing type size on the cover of this newsletter serves as both text and illustration. While perfectly readable, it also provides the reader with a quirky visual diversion—an element that hooks the reader on to the page.

pages 8, frequency Biannually, quantity 3,000, software QuarkXPress, Adobe Photoshop

CalArts
current

NOVEMBER 1991

VOL. X NO. 1

THE FIRST CALIFORNIA SUMMER ARTS SUMMIT

For three days this past July, CalArts hosted the first California Summer Arts Summit which brought together 75 leaders from organizations and representatives from 20 foundations and corporations. The participants in the Summit were perhaps the most diverse cross section of cultural pathfinders ever assembled in California. The event was sponsored by the San Francisco Foundation, the Wallace Alexander Gerbode Foundation, the Irvine Foundation, the Walter and Elise Haas Fund, Mervyn's and the California Arts Council.

CALARTS CURRENT

client
CALIFORNIA INSTITUTE OF THE ARTS

business
ART INSTITUTE

design firm
REVERB

art director/designer
SOMI KIM

photographers
STEVEN A. GUNTHER STEVEN CALLIS

This is an example of intelligent design continuity. Each issue of this tabloid is printed with a different second color. There is also a consistent typographic hierarchy that is complemented by creative photo cropping for variety.

pages 8, frequency 3/academic year, quantity 13,000-15,000, software QuarkXPress, Aldus Freehand

Honor Roll

YOUR GIFTS TO THE ART CENTER ANNUAL FUND ARE AMONG THE MOST IMPORTANT WE RECEIVE. THEY HELP US PAY FOR IMPORTANT THINGS LIKE SCHOLARSHIPS, COMPENSATION FOR FACULTY, AND ADDITIONS TO RESOURCES THAT DIRECTLY IMPROVE THE QUALITY OF STUDENT LIFE AND THEREFORE THE QUALITY OF ART CENTER AS A WHOLE.

BUT ALMOST MORE IMPORTANT, YOUR GIFTS ALLOW ME TO TELL OTHER MAJOR FUNDING SOURCES LIKE CORPORATIONS, FOUNDA- TIONS, AND GOVERNMENT THAT "YES, OUR ALUMNI DO SUPPORT US." WITHOUT YOUR SUPPORT THEY'D IMMEDIATELY (AND RIGHTLY) ASK WHY THEY SHOULD GIVE US MONEY IF OUR OWN GRADUATES DON'T.

SO THANKS FOR YOUR GIFTS. LIKE MOST THINGS ABOUT THE ART CENTER EXPERIENCE. THEY WORK VERY HARD.

DAVID R. BROWN, PRESIDENT

HONOR ROLL 91

client

ART CENTER COLLEGE OF DESIGN

business

ART COLLEGE

design firm

ART CENTER COLLEGE OF DESIGN

art director

REBECA MÉNDEZ

designer

DARREN NAMAYE

photographer

STEVEN A. HELLER

Few tabloid newsletters use both front and back covers exclusively for images—they simply cannot afford the space. But this elegant, curiously abstract photo- graph demands it. Inside, the otherwise monotonous list of names is made into an interesting design through the use of transpar- ent color fields.

pages 6, frequency Once, quantity 10,000, software Macintosh

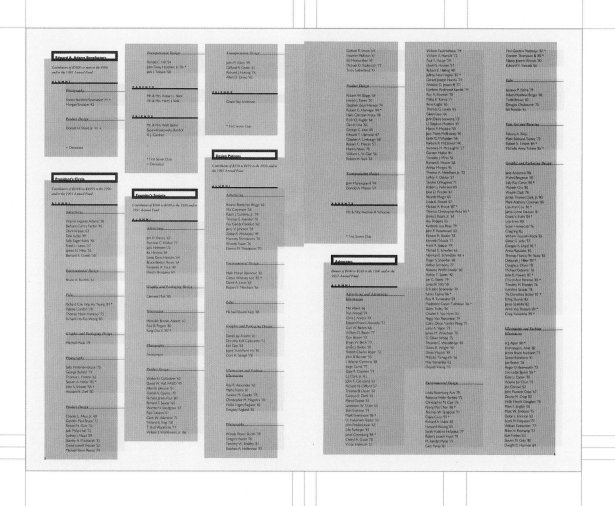

A PUBLICATION FOR ART CENTER ALUMNI, VOLUME 6, NUMBER 1, FALL 1994

art center faces the future of design

ABRIDGED 6

client

ART CENTER COLLEGE OF DESIGN

business

ART COLLEGE

design firm

ART CENTER COLLEGE OF DESIGN

art director

DARIN BEAMAN

designers

CHRIS HAAGA
DARIN BEAMAN

photographers

STEVEN A. HELLER AND OTHERS

The textured paper alone contributes to making this an alluring package. But the new-wave design format is expertly achieved, as it offers the correct balance between text and image.

pages 8, frequency Semiannually, quantity 10,000, software Strata StudioPro, Adobe Photoshop, QuarkXPress

art center faces the future of design

From wrist calculators to guided missiles, digital technology is everywhere and all-pervasive. It's had a vast impact on the way people learn, work, play, and move through this world—even on those who never suspected that they were part of the computer revolution.

With the advent of the PC (personal computer) the technology is now more accessible, allowing more people to become willing experts at communicating, working, and generating ideas via the new technology. The reach of this new phase extends so far that we can neither define its limits nor predict its influence on our lives.

by Alison Goodman

To attempt even a working definition of such a phenomenon is to engage in an unwinnable wrestling match with something that is ever-changing. When Art Center President David R. Brown took office in 1985, he pledged to place this emerging technology at the center of his strategic plan for the college. The digital revolution was then in its infancy. Now, nine years and 130 workstations later, computers continue to broaden the educational experience.

Although apprehension is a natural human response in any time of transformation, there is no sign that Art Center is hesitating in its commitment to explore fully the digital landscape. "The technology is brand new," says Brown, "there is no 'there' to catch up to either on the outside or the inside; there are no old computer experts to rely on for guidance. Aggressive acquisition of the technology to furnish the computer labs allows those that can, and want to, to investigate and experiment with the enormous potential of the new tools. Our strategy is 'build it and they will come.'" So far the plan has paid off. A recent survey requisitioned by Brown and the department chairs of other schools and programs concluded that in the realm of computer education Art Center is "a unique resource in the world."

EIGHTH TERM STUDENT RUSSELL FRACE'S COMPUTER-GENERATED DESIGN OF A SPORTS VEHICLE WITH MOTORCYCLE CHARACTERISTICS FOR BMW.

"The legend that Art Center's first computer lab consisted of two Ataris in a broom closet is not exactly true," muses Computer Graphics Department Chair Rob Henniger (rasd T4). "I was in that class, and we actually had three Ataris. The computers were on a cart, and each day our instructor, Tim Blinn, had to wheel the cart out of the broom closet and hunt for an empty classroom."

Since then almost nine million dollars in corporate contributions of cash, equipment, and software from 41 companies, including Alias Research, Inc., General Motors Corporation, Silicon Graphics, Inc., and SOFTIMAGE, Inc., has built the most sophisticated art and design college computer facility in the country. There are now 130 computer workstations in the 11,000 square feet of the college's new South Wing dedicated to the execution of concepts via digital technology. The roster of equipment has been carefully developed to serve all majors at Art Center: there are 35 Silicon Graphics workstations that provide high-end 3D-animation and modeling capabilities, and 95 Apple Macintosh computers that facilitate photo-imaging, graphic design, and experimentation in the emerging field of interactive media. The labs also include many "peripherals" such as scanning equipment, sound facilities, and video digitizing/output technology. In order to serve the coming wave of interactive projects, Henniger and the college's director of development, Tim Buffie, are working to acquire equipment for mastering CD ROMs.

Some of those who have come as corporate sponsors eager to see what innovative minds can bring to the new technology. Students in all majors are applying computers to both their personal visions and to the inquiries of industry leaders. This past year BMW sponsored a project that required students to design a new sport vehicle exclusively on the computer. The results were exciting—not only because design points were successfully addressed—but also because new representations observed and participated in a bit of Art Center history. For the first time in the college's 60 years of transportation design, this project did not employ the tried and true method of clay modeling. While complete abandonment of the clay plates was an important experiment, the computer will not necessarily replace traditional processes as much as it will augment other tools and techniques. This hybridization of methods is evident throughout the school. Students in all departments flow seamlessly back and forth between the linear thought involved in the mastery of digital technology and the analogical reasoning that has always characterized the intuitive expressions of artists and designers. Most impressed with the newly acquired skills of our students are their department chairs. "It's amazing to watch," says Photographic Chair Tim Bradley (rasd '81). "The students are both visually sensitive and entirely unafraid of the electronics. They see the integration as natural." A recent experience with Kodak illustrates his point. Eager to see student applications of their new digital camera, the people at Kodak were surprised to learn that some of the students' work utilized features of the camera that Kodak considered limitations or anomalies of their product. The current display of 10x10 student work at the company's headquarters in Rochester, New York, not only demonstrates the camera's capabilities but also suggests that there are many exciting new areas waiting to be discovered.

As the "digital blizzard" continues to blur distinctions among creative disciplines, interdepartmental collaborations are becoming more common at Art Center. A recent Apple Computer Inc. open competition asked college design students nationwide to develop an interface for the InterNet. Apple awarded the prize for the Best Visual Design to the "Library of Babel," a collaboration between Art Center Illustration major Taylor Wescoatt and Alec Bernstein (rasd '94). Their entry relied on right brain cues such as shapes, sounds, and images for navigation along "the information highway." Also recognized for their collaborative efforts in the realm of digital media were Kent Campbell (rasd '93), Brian Dorsey (rasd '93), Matthew Neri (rasd '93), John Grimsing (rasd '94), and Dinz Trinkin (rasd '94) for their design, production, and presentation of an interactive, multimedia catalog about Art Center. I.D. magazine honored their efforts with its Design Distinction award this past

THE GENERAL MOTORS COMPUTER GRAPHICS LABORATORY AT ART CENTER: A LONG WAY FROM "NO ATARIS IN A BROOM CLOSET."

2

IS YOUR CAR STALLED ON THE INFORMATION HIGHWAY?

First experiences in the realm of the digital can be daunting. Art Center instructor, graduate advisor, and new media critic Peter Lunenfeld suggests the following resources for those interested in getting up to speed:

REQUIRED READING MACHINES

Wired: A monthly publication for those interested in the cultural impact of the computer revolution.

New Media: Monthly with editorial emphasis on the tools of the trade.

In addition, subscribe to a publication directed to your specific platform, such as Mac World or Macuser for Macintosh patrons, and Byte or PC World for IBM users.

CONVENTIONS

Attending a convention can be overwhelming at first. Go anyway. Wander around; talk to people. After the first few, you will be navigating the high-tech conventions like an old pro. If you are still not convinced that it's worth the effort, keep this in mind: conventions provide great venues in which to buy software at steep discounts!

Southern California often hosts meetings that address the cutting edge of computer technology. The recommended annual meetings in the Los Angeles area are: Digital World and Show Biz Expo. In San Francisco the annual Mac World convention is recommended. The most advanced conference in the world dealing with graphics and interactive media is the SIGGRAPH (Special Interest Group Graphics) Conference, which has previously convened at points all over the globe and will meet in Los Angeles in 1995.

abridged

TANSEY'S TURN

PAINTER MARK TANSEY'S WORK
IS CURRENTLY FEATURED IN A MAJOR
MUSEUM RETROSPECTIVE.
A PROFILE OF THE ARTIST BEGINS ON PAGE 4.

A Publication for Art Center Alumni, Volume 4, Number 1, Fall 1993

ABRIDGED 4

client

ART CENTER COLLEGE
OF DESIGN

business

ART COLLEGE

design firm

ART CENTER COLLEGE
OF DESIGN

art director

REBECA MÉNDEZ

designer

MARY CAY WALP

photographers

STEVEN A. HELLER
AND OTHERS

This horizontal tabloid cover
adds drama to this publication. Inside the still life and
object photographs are also
dramatized when, as silhou-
ettes, they are given a sense
of movement. Color blocks
and reverse type also give
this a spritely feeling.

pages 8, frequency
Semiannually, quantity
10,000, software
Macintosh

BOB WEBB (TRAN '83X)

POSITION: Consultant, H. N. and Frances C. Berger Foundation (provides grants to civic and educational programs, primarily in Southern California). **DESIGN CREDITS:** Automotive concepts for the movies Knightrider and Robocop with noted entertainment designer George Barris, coordinator of high profile alternative fuel vehicle project at Art Center and Art Center (Europe) sponsored by the Berger Foundation. **MAJOR INTERESTS:** Research, educational funding. **PRESENT PROJECT:** Collaboration with Barris on automobile designs for Hollywood production.

In the transportation design project at Art Center's two campuses, we wanted, through the publicity, to give the public an idea of what they'll be driving in the year 2000. It helped the students immeasurably, and their ideas were realistic. I find the postal van a very workable solution for today. It could be applied to a wide variety of services. Eventually the push for alternative fuel sources would have appeared because of miniaturization and the public outcry for solutions to pollution. But without government intervention it wouldn't have become the prominent issue it is right now. So the market is there, but it's very limited. Government must be supportive the whole way, and that support will be strengthened by the increase and exposure of private research efforts. I'd like to see more lecture programs at schools like Art Center which address all aspects of alternative energy sources. There's real power in going into Art Center's library and watching tapes of lectures from various experts. That's the way to document where we are today, so that in 10 or 20 years we can see who was right.

ZERO-EMISSIONS VEHICLES ON THE FAST TRACK

THREE ALUMNI DISCUSS ALTERNATIVE ENERGY VEHICLES

HARDLY A DAY GOES BY AT THE PASADENA CAMPUS
WHEN THE WORDS "ALTERNATIVE ENERGY VEHICLES"
AREN'T SPOKEN. THE RACE TO FIND THE FLAWLESS FUEL
HAS BEEN SPURRED BY CALIFORNIA LEGISLATION, CALL-
ING FOR 2 PERCENT OF AUTOMAKERS' SALES IN THE
STATE TO BE OF ZERO-EMISSIONS VEHICLES (ZEVS) BY
1998. AT LEAST ONE-THIRD OF THE NATION'S STATES ARE
EXPECTED TO FOLLOW SUIT. CONSEQUENTLY ALUMNI
AND STUDENTS ALIKE HAVE PLUNGED INTO POWER
TECHNOLOGY RESEARCH TO FIND VIABLE SOLUTIONS
FOR TOMORROW'S ENVIRONMENTALLY FRIENDLY VEHI-
CLES, BOTH FOR PERSONAL USE AND FOR MASS TRANSIT.
ABRIDGED INTERVIEWED THREE ALUMNI WHO HAVE
PURSUED DIFFERENT AREAS OF THE ALTERNATIVE
TRANSPORTATION INDUSTRY TO GET THEIR VIEWS ON
MASS TRANSIT, ELECTRIC TECHNOLOGY, AND GOVERN-
MENT SUPPORT. —ANN BURNHAM

Insight

1. An electric college commuter car by student Jung Kim, designed to transport students at large universities to classes and nearby shopping centers (Berger project).
2. An electric mail truck designed by student Kelly Wright (Berger project).
3. Ron Powers's design for a mass-transit vehicle adaptable to various types of rail systems.
4. Built by Amerigon and PAID CALSTARTS Showcase Electric Vehicle (SEV), for which Bruce Severance served as principal designer.

RON POWERS (TRAN '71)

POSITION: Owner, Powers Design International, Newport Beach, California. **DESIGN CREDITS:** 1989 Cadillac El Dorado, the two cars produced by India's state-run automobile industry, manned space station "Freedom"; transit vehicles for various kinds of rail systems. **MAJOR INTEREST:** Pneumatic- or air-powered transit system. **PRESENT PROJECT:** Working on one of four teams chosen by the federal government to design a national system for high speed magnetic levitation trains.

"When cities start to look into mass transit, they look at extensions, guideways, road acquisition costs, and power systems, and they realize that it's going to cost $50 to $100 million a mile. Then they close the books, because they don't have $50 to $100 million a mile." I've looked the world over for affordable power technology, and I've tried to talk up this pneumatic power system to cities and counties in need of rapid transit. (An air-powered system is currently running in a public park in Indonesia. The operating cost is less than $1 per passenger, per day.) People sit on freeways and surface streets gridlocked and say, 'We need a monorail. Well, we've got a great bus system in Los Angeles right now, and nobody rides it. If your system doesn't get people to and from the station, it's not going to be used." "Five years ago I started seeing some renewed interest in mass transit. People were finally gridlocked enough to say, 'Please, we need some help.' Well, as a transportation designer and not just a car designer, I think I can do that. There are alternatives out there. It's all about compromise. My job is to find a compromise people will make."

BRUCE SEVERANCE (TRAN '90)

POSITION: Designer, Amerigon Inc. (aimed at redirecting the aerospace industry to transportation technology). **DESIGN CREDITS:** Principal designer of Showcase Electric Vehicle, in collaboration with alumni Larry Rodgers (TRAN '77) and David Heller (PROD '74), author of "Instant Electric Refueling" in Sunworld, Journal of the International Solar Energy Society; development of educational curricula on solar power for schools nationwide (grades 3 to 12) and an environmental ethics for Art Center. **MAJOR INTEREST:** Solar thermal power. **PRESENT PROJECT:** Amerigon's Neighborhood Electric Vehicle.

"There is a niche market for electric vehicles that exists today—to sell affordably to 3 to 5 percent of the population, specifically families that already have a couple of cars in the garage. I have a hard time understanding why no one is seizing the opportunity faster, because I really believe that if American companies don't do it, foreign companies will. And we may lose both a good market and an opportunity to boost our economy. "Even if the power is coming from fossil fuels, electricity is cleaner than gasoline. And electric technology is always moving toward a cleaner state. It's easier to control a generating source than it is to control six million tail pipes. "With the advancement of technology making it increasingly possible to transfer energy from coast to coast, I envision the country eventually converting to solar power for stationary sources of electricity and eventually for moving vehicles." "I don't think it's something that is on the fringe anymore. There's a mainstream of people who are extremely concerned about the environment. "As designers we are enormously empowered. We owe it to ourselves, society, and posterity always to consider the potential of our choices."

8 9

THIS
THE NUTS AND BOLTS
EDITION

MIT. The name conjures up lots of images: of engineers, scientists, and computers; of academic excellence, intellectual challenges, demanding workload, and all-nighters. But we'd like you to see those images a bit differently. MIT does indeed have the best engineering program in the nation (see **US News & World Report**) and is a leader in science education, but we also offer exceptional opportunities in fields ranging from architec-ture to literature, economics to music, management to philosophy. And though it's certainly a tough school, envision instead getting value for your money—in the form of stimulating courses taught by some of the brightest people in the world, unparalleled opportunities to do research that matters, and wide open career paths.

Over the next few months you'll be receiving piles of mail from the other great colleges and universities (and you haven't heard the last from us), so we've designed this piece to give you some early insight into MIT. We'd like to show you what MIT has to offer you as a fresh-man and to guide you through the application process. We won't overwhelm you with breathless descriptions of the place, nor try to anticipate every one of your questions. You can get the full picture from the rest of our literature, from talking to people here at the Institute (all you have to do is call 617 253-4791), and from a campus visit.

Take advantage of those resources to get to know us. We think you'll be surprised at how many different images grace our halls.

MIT INSIGHT

client

MASSACHUSETTS
INSTITUTE OF
TECHNOLOGY/
ADMISSIONS

business

UNIVERSITY

design firm

SHEPARD/QURAESHI
ASSOCIATES

art director

SAMINA QURAESHI

designer

TANIA LIEPMANN

photographer

JIM DOW

This four-color tabloid is both restrained and exuber-ant. The color alternately serves as a frame and accent for its content. The otherwise mundane cover image used in this context is a witty blend of information and graphics.

pages 8, frequency Annually, quantity 55,000, software QuarkXPress

CATALYST

client

ILLINOIS INSTITUTE OF
TECHNOLOGY

business

UNIVERSITY

design firm

ESSEX TWO

art director/
designer

NANCY DENNEY ESSEX

illustrator

WILL NORTHERNER

Web printing allows for larger print runs at less expense. However, the quality often suffers. This one-color tabloid printed on web offset 50-pound stock takes advan-tage of the limitations, using high-contrast illustrations.

pages 12-16, frequency Quarterly, quantity 45,000, software QuarkXPress

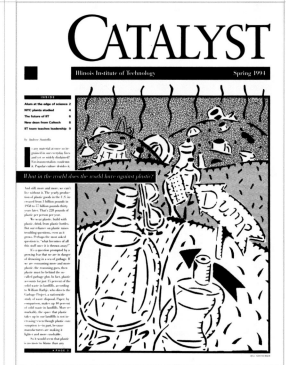

F. I. T. NETWORK

client

FASHION INSTITUTE OF TECHNOLOGY

business

UNIVERSITY

design firm

RICHARD DANNE & ASSOCIATES

art director

RICHARD DANNE

designer

GAYLE SHIMOUN

Here the impact of silhouetted photographs are strengthened by the deliberate and radical changes in scale. While the logo and format are constant, the layouts change from issue to issue and page to page.

pages 16, frequency Quarterly, quantity 10,000, software QuarkXPress, Adobe Illustrator

Published for faculty, staff, alumni, and friends of the Fashion Institute of Technology

Page 3
Scholar Takes Up "Residence" at F.I.T.

Volume Three, Number Three, Spring 1993

Page 4
Experts Agree: "CIM-ple" Standards Significant for Industry

Page 11
Students Put Shoe Designs through Paces in Footwear Competition

Page 8
Jaffe Sews Up Distinguished Career

Page 14
Alumna Packs Panache in Paper Creations

NEWSLETTER

LITTLE RED SCHOOL HOUSE AND ELISABETH IRWIN HIGH SCHOOL

Winter 1993

More than 75 stars of stage and screen from our Lower and Middle School sang with Peter, Paul and Mary at the Brooklyn Academy of Music for an upcoming PBS program. Congratulations — you were all great! Look for this special concert in March 1993.

ANNOUNCEMENT!

Elisabeth Irwin High School is one of 13 independent schools in the nation to receive a recent grant from the DeWitt Wallace-Reader's Digest Fund's Independent School Opportunity Program. This prestigious award program focuses on increased diversity of students and faculty, as well as support for collaborative public-private projects, in independent schools.

The three-year restricted grant to EI for $307,000 will advance the school's efforts to increase the representation of teachers of color on the faculty, through the establishment of an Associate Teacher Program. The grant will also support the development and publication of our Urban Studies Curriculum

as a model program for high school study. Mike Lockett, Director of Urban Studies, developed this curriculum and will implement this aspect of the grant.

"The entire school community is immensely pleased to have received this grant," said Director Andrew McLaren. "This recognition by the DeWitt Wallace-Reader's Digest Fund is a most positive endorsement of the exceptional qualities of Elisabeth Irwin High School. Although the award may only be used for the specific program initiatives of the grant, we believe it will serve as a powerful impetus to our current efforts to raise vital operating revenues through the 5-year Fund for the High School campaign."

FROM THE DIRECTOR

Sixty years ago, one hundred and sixty-five pupils attended the opening classes at the Little Red School House at 196 Bleecker Street. Tuition was $125 a year. Lunches were extra. So was June Camp, $1.00 a day.

Some things change — but not everything. The same year, 1932, one of our publications stated: "The ideal of the school will be to have the children live and work in a cooperative rather than competitive atmosphere. The teacher will strive to be an influential member of the group but not to dominate it. The learning process will take place through experiencing first-hand or vicariously rather than through being taught."

We continue to believe that the focus is the classroom should be on the learner, rather than the teacher. So I was delighted to read in *The Wall Street Journal* recently about a "new wave of teachers... preaching a new creed of student engagement... They stress process before product, active learning, and constructing meaning rather than developing skills. Taking their inspirations from learning theorists such as Jean Piaget and John Dewey, they seek to develop the 'whole child,' morals and all...It is a grand and risky experiment."

This year's restatement of our school mission concludes: "The progressive ideals that in 1921 gave life and inspiration to the school — academic excellence and creativity, active learning and innovative teaching, respect for the individual and responsibility to the community — continue to guide the school today." It remains a grand venture — but it is no longer all that risky, or even experimental, because we now have a large and growing body of proof that it works.

Our daily quest is of course to make it work better. One of the dangers in this regard is to set up "either-or" constructs, which allow only one option. For instance, the Journal comment quoted above refers to "constructing meanings rather than developing skills." Skills, by any reasonable description, assist in the construction of meanings, and understood meanings in turn motivate the development of skills. The two are not opposites, but go hand in hand.

I did not split hairs about this, however, in a letter of response to the Journal. I merely pointed out that Elisabeth Irwin's educational beliefs and ideals had weathered many a storm these past few decades: it was good to see them now held in such high esteem. Elisabeth Irwin was ahead of her time in stating that a good education was not just a matter of conveying a body of knowledge from teacher to learner. It was also about providing tools for future learning, including — indeed especially — learning how to cope with change. This simply cannot be done other than in a classroom which focuses attention on the learner rather than the teacher. Our founder was far ahead of her time in seeing this.

ANDREW McLAREN
Director

LITTLE RED SCHOOL HOUSE & ELISABETH IRWIN HIGH SCHOOL NEWSLETTER

client

LITTLE RED SCHOOL HOUSE & ELISABETH IRWIN HIGH SCHOOL

business

PRIVATE ELEMENTARY/HIGH SCHOOL

design firm

LEAH LOCOCO

art director/ designer

LEAH LOCOCO

In this two-color standard-format newsletter, information in the form of short takes is packed in a readable mélange. Candid snapshots are the predominant form of illustration.

pages 8, frequency Quarterly, quantity 5,000, software QuarkXPress

NEWSLETTER

client

UNIVERSITY OF
CALIFORNIA, SAN
DIEGO SCHOOL OF
ARCHITECTURE

business

UNIVERSITY

design firm

REVERB

art director

LORRAINE WILD

designers

SUSAN PARR
ANDREA FELLA

photographer

ALAN DECKER

The long narrow shape may at first seem difficult to read, but in fact adds to the delight of the entire design. The typeface is a revival of Copperplate, which suggests an old/new aesthetic. The logo smartly cuts into the cover image making it a changing element of an otherwise consistent masthead.

pages 12, frequency Quarterly, quantity 7,000, software QuarkXPress

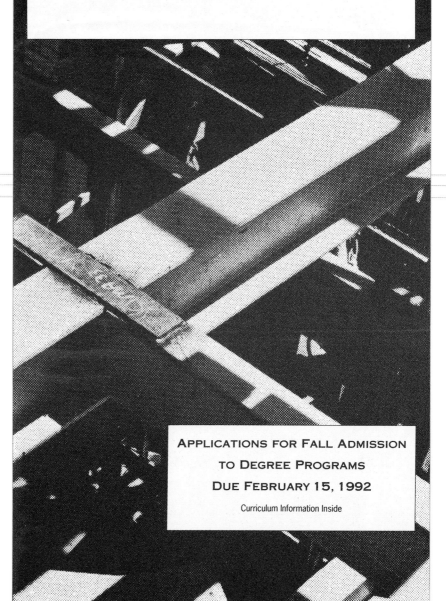

CONTENTS

See page 7 for Quick Facts about the UCSD School of Architecture.

UNIVERSITY OF CALIFORNIA, SAN DIEGO
SCHOOL OF ARCHITECTURE

VOLUME 2, NO.2

NEWSLETTER

APPLICATIONS FOR FALL ADMISSION

TO DEGREE PROGRAMS

DUE FEBRUARY 15, 1992

Curriculum Information Inside

See page 6 for a drawing of
Hodgetts-Fung's design for a new
temporary library at UCLA.

UNIVERSITY OF CALIFORNIA, SAN DIEGO
SCHOOL OF ARCHITECTURE

VOLUME 2, No. 3

NEWSLETTER

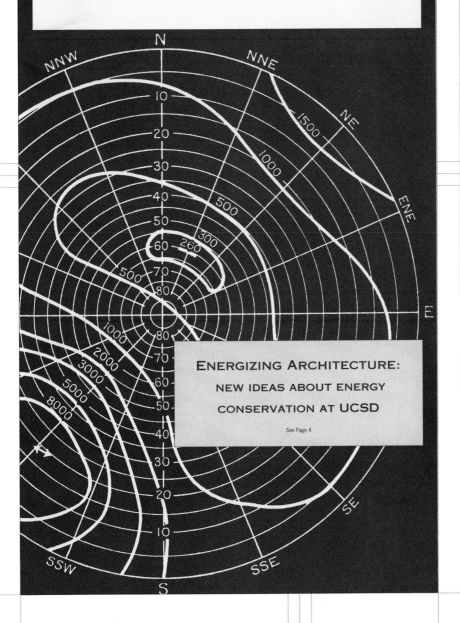

ENERGIZING ARCHITECTURE:

NEW IDEAS ABOUT ENERGY

CONSERVATION AT UCSD

See Page 4

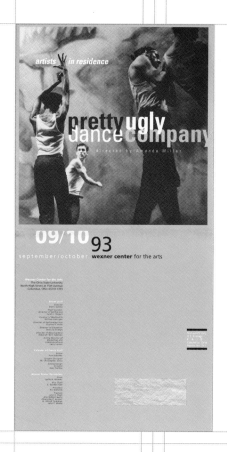

WEXNER CENTER
CALENDAR OF
EVENTS/NEWSLETTER

c l i e n t

WEXNER CENTER FOR
THE ARTS

b u s i n e s s

CONTEMPORARY ARTS
CENTER

d e s i g n   f i r m

WEXNER CENTER
DESIGN DEPARTMENT

a r t   d i r e c t o r

GARY SANKEY

d e s i g n e r

M. CHRISTOPHER
JONES

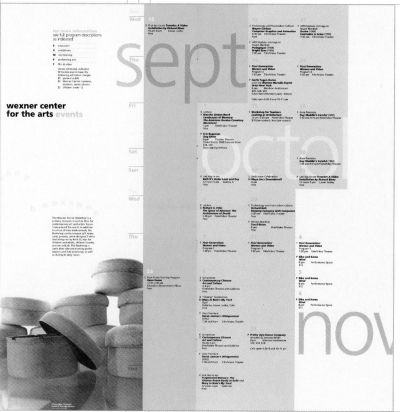

This long and narrow, folded-in-half calendar of events uses two colors (the second changes with each issue). While the interiors are more or less consistent with the governing format, the cover photographs and headline treatment also change from one issue to the next.

pages 12, frequency Bimonthly, quantity 12,000, software QuarkXPress, Aldus Freehand, Adobe Photoshop

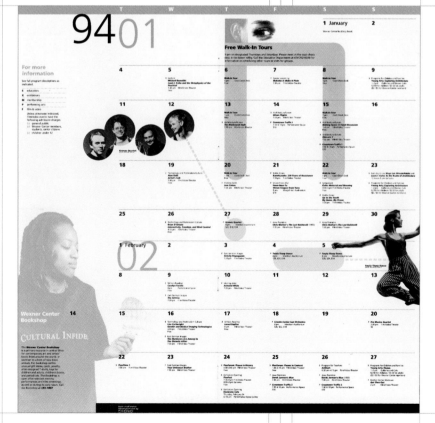

ALTERNATIVES

client

**THE CONTEMPORARY
ARTS CENTER**

business

ART MUSEUM

design firm

LAMSON DESIGN

art director

DALE LAMSON

designer

LAMSON DESIGN

photographers

JANEY BIGGS *(left)*
KEITH HADLEY *(right)*

Every issue of this two-color
tabloid has a radically different design. This approach
requires the full-time maintenance of a designer, but
the exciting graphic results
are well worth the effort.

pages Varies, frequency
5/year, quantity 4,500-6,000,
software QuarkXPress,
Adobe Illustrator

CONTEMPORARY

ALTERNATIVES

CENTER

VOLUME
3

Songs of My People ★ Sculptural Concerns: Contemporary American Metalworking ★ Super Sundays During Songs

ISSUE
5

CALENDAR OF EVENTS

client

GOETHE HOUSE, NEW YORK/GERMAN CULTURAL CENTER

business

CULTURAL CENTER

design firm

D•SIGN HAUS

designers

KERSTIN BACH KARIN KAUTZKY ELKE SCHULZ

photographer

UDO SPREITZENBARTH

This two-color, narrow pamphlet-styled newsletter, a listing of events and programs, is layered with type and images depicting the films and exhibitions on hand. Continued on pages 62 and 63.

pages 16, frequency 3/year, quantity 12,000, software QuarkXPress, Adobe Photoshop

GOETHE HOUSE

NEW YORK

German Cultural Center

concept: DSign Haus, NY 212:777 83 00

GOETHE HOUSE NEW YORK

German **C**ultural **C**enter
1014 Fifth Avenue
New York **NY** 10028
212. **439 8700**

APRIL
MAY
JUNE
1994

CONCERT 1 • May 19 • **Morton Feldman** • **Patterns in a Chromatic Field** (1981) • Michael Bach, cello • Anthony de Mare, piano

CONCERT 2 • May 22 • **John Cage** • **Ophelia** (1946) • **The Wonderful Widow of Eighteen Springs** (1942) • **Nowth Upon Nacht** (1984) • **ONE** 5 (1990) Anthony de Mare, piano

ONE 13 (1992) **(U.S. PREMIERE)** Michael Bach, cello

Intermission • Michael **Bach Bachtischa C-A-G-E 1** (1993) (U.S. PREMIERE) Michael Bach, cello • **Bernd Alois Zimmermann** • **Intercomunicazione** (1967) (U.S. PREMIERE) Michael Bach, cello Anthony de Mare, piano

CONCERT 1 Goethe House New York German Cultural Center 1014 Fifth Avenue at 82nd Street. Free Admission. **7:00** p.m.

CONCERT 2 The Kathryn Bache Miller Theatre, B'way at 116th Street. Tickets $ 15 general admission, $ 5 students and seniors Box Office 854 **77**99. **8:00** p.m.

Goethe House New York / German Cultural Center presents two concerts of contemporary music by John Cage and others

M U S I C

featuring German cellist Michael Bach and American pianist Anthony de Mare. The concerts are part of the Citycircus, the program of events in tandem with an exhibition on John Cage at the Guggenheim Museum SoHo. Cellist **Michael Bach** is an adventurer and explorer in the field of music, doing deliberate experiments with and on his cello. Bach's avant-garde virtuousity prepared for premiere performances of composers such as Feldman, Lachenmann, Schoenberg, Walter Zimmermann, and most recently, John Cage. He first demonstrated his Cello Curved Bow to John Cage in 1990. Thereafter, Bach and Cage worked together on the compositions ONE 8, **Ryoanji for Cello** and ONE 13.

Pianist Anthony de Mare has received many honors, including First Prize at the 1983 International Compet -ition of Contemporary Piano Music in France and both First Prize and Audience Prize at the 1982 International Gaudeamus Interpreters Com -petition in the Netherlands. New works have been written for de Mare by composers Biscardi, Monk, Zorn, Boehmer, and Wolff, to name a few.

De Mare's first full solo recording, featuring works by John Cage and Meredith Monk and entitled **Pianos and Voices**, was released in 1992.

Film

GERMAN COMEDY: EAST MEETS WEST

Goethe House September 19-27 Unification gave German filmmakers from East and West the opportunity to explore the division of Germany with irony, wit and humor. This series presents film comedies dealing with the situations of people who lived right next to each other but were still so far apart.

Sept.19 at 6:00 p.m. & Sept.20 at 8:00 p.m. **GO TRABI GO**, 1991, by Peter Timm, color, 96 min. The Struutz family from Bitterfeld near Leipzig is looking forward to realizing their lifelong dream of tracing Goethe's famous journey to Italy. The actual hero of the "classical trail" turns out to be the car, the Trabant or Trabi, which provides more than just transportation.

Sept.19 at 8:00 p.m. & Sept.22 at 6:00 p.m. **THE CONFESSION**, (Die Beichte), 1990, by Joachim Kuhn, color, 10 min. On the doorstep to eternal salvation or damnation, former East German leader Erich Honecker makes his confession to the Pope. **HALLO COMRADE**, (Grüß Gott, Genosse), 1993 by Manfred Stelzer, color, 88 min. Adolf Wendler, formerly an ambitious and determined teacher in the GDR, appears to adjust extremely well to the changed demands of the post-Wall situation: With the right political party and the right outfit he is accepted into the Bavarian school system. Everything runs smoothly until one day a student from the past catches up with him...

Sept.20 at 6:00 p.m. & Sept.23 at 8:00 p.m. **NO MORE MR. NICE GUY**, (Wir können auch anders), 1992, by Detlev Buck, color, 92 min. Never did the future seem so promising to slightly retarded Kipp and his taciturn brother Most with the notarized certificate of his inheritance in their pocket - neither of them can read or write - and a wreath for Grandma's grave, they set off in an old truck in search of Wendelohe, Grandma's estate in East Germany...

Sept. 22 at 8:00 p.m.& Sept.27 at 6:00 p.m. **TWO TO ONE**, (Zwei zu eins), 1991, by Riki Kalbe, color, 3 min. Playing with images of legs and high heels from East and West, this short film pays attention to colors, shapes and symbols. **THE LYING GAME**, (Wer zweimal lügt), 1993, by Bertram von Boxberg, color, 81 min. Two old people meet, both have unfulfilled dreams: He, a legal bookseller, always wanted to be a judge, she, a housekeeper, wants to marry her employer, the President of the Senate. With a telephone call from the Minister of Justice who is looking for retired judges for the reconstruction of East Germany, those dreams might just come true...

Sept. 23 at 6:00 p.m. & Sept.27 at 8:00 p.m. **RISING TO THE BAIT,** (Der Brocken), 1991, by Vadim Glowna, color, 97 min. The widow Ada Fenske shares her house with the daughter of a former party secretary in one of the most beautiful coastal spots of the island of Rügen. Her property is next to a Soviet military installation which West Germans want to take over. Ada quickly learns to enjoy the capitalist ways by warding off the waves of would-be buyers. In the end it is love that decides the fate of her house, not money.

Expanding on the 1994 German Federal election, Goethe House New York has invited **Michael Schomers** to present and discuss his recently finished film focussing on rightwing parties, one of the most volatile topics in the current political debate. The filmmakers accompanied leading figures of the extreme right during the election campaign, documenting the ambivalence of their demagogical promises.

Oct. 13 at 7:00p.m.
GERMANY FOR THE GERMANS - The Rightwing Radicals and their Electoral Promises, (Deutschland den Deutschen - Die Rechtsradikalen iund hre Wahlversprechen), 1994, by Wolfgang Landgräber and Michael Schomers, color, 43 min., in German (with English subtitles)

NEWS + EVENTS

client

THE FRANKLIN INSTITUTE SCIENCE MUSEUM

business

MUSEUM

design firm

ALLEMANN/ALMQUIST + JONES

art director

HANS-U. ALLEMANN

designers

GREG PAONE
STEPHEN SHAKLEFORD

photographer

MARK TUSCHMAN

pages 4, frequency Quarterly, quantity 20,000, software Aldus PageMaker, Adobe Illustrator, Adobe Photoshop

CALENDAR

client

THE J. PAUL GETTY MUSEUM

business

MUSEUM

design firm

J. PAUL GETTY TRUST PUBLICATION SERVICES

art director

DEENIE YUDELL

designer

LESLIE FITCH

photographers

CHARLES PASSELA
JACK ROSS
AND OTHERS

Quiet elegance is what makes this schedule of exhibitions appealing to the eye. Like a mini-poster, this full-color cover provides visual stimulation and information, too.

pages Foldout, frequency Quarterly, quantity 85,000

A Season ## at the Gardner

AUTUMN 1991 · VOLUME I · NUMBER I

Center detail of the largest textile in the exhibition. Wrap or cover, Indian, 1850–1900 ➤

World of Textiles

Sumptuous textiles originating from eleven countries and spanning six centuries are now on display in the Gardner's temporary exhibition space. Entitled *Exploring the Treasures of the Isabella Stewart Gardner Museum II: Introducing the World of Textiles*, the exhibition will remain on view through January 5, 1992. According to Ada H. Logan, conservator at the Museum and curator of the exhibition, "Each of these pieces is exquisite. Yet they represent only a sampling of all the marvelous textiles displayed by Isabella throughout the Museum."

Several beautiful pieces have been brought out of storage especially for this exhibition, including a Caucasian carpet that once graced the Beacon Street residence where Isabella Stewart Gardner lived prior to Fenway Court. Among other objects of historic interest are a needle lace said to have belonged to Marie Antoinette, and a table cover crocheted at the edge by Mrs. Gardner with her first name in the pattern.

This exhibition is the second in a series of special exhibitions focusing upon aspects of the collection. The series provides opportunities to re-examine works of art in novel and stimulating contexts, distinct from the unique settings of the galleries.

An exhibition catalogue with 72 black-and-white illustrations and diagrams is on sale in the Museum Shop. Members are invited to attend the curator's gallery talk on the textiles on Saturday, October 19 at 2:30.

A spiderweb of safety netting covers the courtyard during renovations this summer.

Ada Logan, curator of the textile exhibition

Speaking Curatorially:

An Interview with Hilliard Goldfarb

Hilliard Goldfarb, the Museum's chief curator, came to the Gardner last January. Dr. Goldfarb had previously served as the first curator for European Art at Dartmouth College's Hood Museum of Art. Other positions he has held include assistant curator of drawings at the Cleveland Museum of Art, assistant professor at Case Western Reserve University, and assistant to the drawings curator at

Harvard's Fogg Museum. His most recent exhibition, entitled *From Fontainebleau to the Louvre*, on French 17th-century art, traveled last year to the Cleveland Museum of Art, the Fogg, and the National Gallery of Canada. His numerous publications include catalogues and articles on Callot, Goya, Jacopo Bellini, Rembrandt, Claude Lorrain, Poussin, Titian, and Boucher. *(continued on page 6)*

A SEASON AT THE GARDNER

client

ISABELLA STEWART GARDNER MUSEUM

business

ART MUSEUM

design firm

SHEPARD/QURAESHI ASSOCIATES

art director

SAMINA QURAESHI

designers

BRYCE AMBO TANIA LIEPMANN

photographer

JOHN KENNARD

This two-color tabloid printed on off-white stock uses a generous number of art and news photographs to announce the events and goals of this museum.

pages 8, frequency Biannually, quantity 1,500, software QuarkXPress

---

THE ART MUSEUM PRINCETON UNIVERSITY NEWSLETTER

client

THE ART MUSEUM, PRINCETON UNIVERSITY

business

ART MUSEUM

design firm

WHITEHOUSE & COMPANY

designer

ROGER WHITEHOUSE

photographers

BRUCE M. WHITE PRINCETON UNIVERSITY STAFF PHOTOGRAPHERS

This two-color, six-page foldout is based on a three-column grid in the traditional manner. A cut of Garamond is used to signify the seriousness of this publication.

pages 6, frequency 3/year, quantity 3,000, software Aldus PageMaker

---

The Art Museum Princeton University

Exhibition of Classical Art to Open Fall Season

The fall exhibition season opens at The Art Museum with the Friends private viewing on September 18 of "Goddess and Polis: The Panathenaic Festival in Ancient Athens" and "Ancient Athens: Photographs by Alison Frantz," both on view from August 31 through November 28.

Organized by the Hood Museum of Art at Dartmouth College, "Goddess and Polis" has been made possible in part by grants from the National Endowment for the Humanities and the National Endowment for the Arts, federal agencies. The exhibition at Princeton is supported by a gift from Gregory Callimanopulos, Class of 1957, with an additional grant from the National Endowment for the Arts.

"Goddess and Polis" is the first exhibition to focus on the rich array of classical art associated with the Panathenaia, the most famous

*Greek, Attic, ca. 500 B.C.
Black-figure Panathenaic amphora
Ceramic, H. 65.5 cm
Bequest of Mrs. Allan Marquand*

religious and civic festival of ancient Athens. Every summer the citizens of Athens moved in solemn procession to the Acropolis to offer a new *peplos*, a richly woven robe, to the cult statue of Athena Polias. It is this procession that many scholars have identified with the famous sculpted frieze on the Parthenon.

The nearly seventy objects in the exhibition, many of which have never been on public display, date generally from the sixth and fifth centuries B.C. and are lent by over thirty-five museums and private collectors. The works include painted Attic vases, silver coins, and sculptures in bronze, marble, and terracotta. Among the most impressive pieces are seven Panathenaic prize amphoras, large vessels that contained the olive oil awarded to victors in the athletic, equine, and musical competitions held every four years at the "Greater" Panathenaia, when the annual festival was celebrated with special pomp. Many of the vases and sculptures represent Athena, the patron deity of the city, while others depict musicians, sacrifices, processions, and athletic events: running, boxing, wrestling, horse and chariot racing, and throwing

the discus and the javelin.

The curator of the exhibition is Jenifer Neils, associate professor and chair of the Department of Art at Case Western Reserve University, Cleveland, and a graduate alumna of the Department of Art and Archaeology at Princeton. Professor Neils is among the speakers participating in a symposium, *Parthenon and Panathenaia*, Saturday, September 18, sponsored by The Art Museum, the Department of Art and Archaeology, the Program in the Ancient World, and the Program in Hellenic Studies under the auspices of the Stanley J. Seeger Fund. The symposium is free and open to the public, but seating will be limited. For information, call The Art Museum at (609) 258-3788, or the Department of Art and Archaeology at (609) 258-3782.

Complementing the treasures on view in "Goddess and Polis" is a smaller but no less fascinating exhibition, "Ancient Athens: Photographs by Alison Frantz." A renowned classical archaeologist and authority on the Late Antique and Early Byzantine periods in Athens, Princeton resident Alison Frantz is famous also for her photographs of Greek monuments, especially those of Athens. The photographs have been selected for the exhibition, with particular emphasis on the goddess Athena, the Parthenon frieze, and other monuments of the Acropolis.

*Alison Frantz, American, born 1903
Parthenon, north frieze slab XVII
Gelatin silver print*

Spring/
Summer
1993

Newsletter

The Contemporary

Pure Beauty: Some

Recent Work from

Los Angeles · Richard

Wilson · Margaret

Honda ·

merican Center
in Paris

Alternating 1 to 100 and

vice versa by Alighiero

e Boetti · Hirokazu

Kosaka: In the Mood ·

rt Talks a
current exhibitions

Installations: Selections

from the Permanent

Collection · "Me"

hater's installation in Pure Beauty

by John Fleck

THE CONTEMPORARY

client

THE MUSEUM OF CONTEMPORARY ART, LOS ANGELES

business

ART MUSEUM

design firm

THE MUSEUM OF CONTEMPORARY ART, LOS ANGELES

designer

CINDY ESTES

photographer

ERIC KOYAMA

This cross between a magazine and newsletter employs a considerable amount of color; two colors are used throughout as well as a full-color cover and center spread. Despite such exuberance, a strict format is maintained in each issue.

pages 16, frequency Quarterly, quantity 20,000, software QuarkXPress

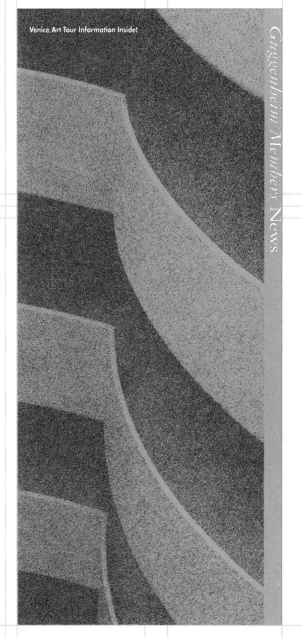

Venice Art Tour Information Inside!

Guggenheim Members News

GUGGENHEIM MEMBERS NEWS

client

SOLOMON R. GUGGENHEIM MUSEUM

business

ART MUSEUM

design firm

GUGGENHEIM MUSEUM SOHO

art director/ designer

MICHELLE MARTINO

photographer

DAVID HEALD

This two-color, accordion-folded newsletter relies on a generous number of surprints to give it the sense of excitement and variety warranted by the museum program.

pages 12, frequency Quarterly, quantity 10,000, software QuarkXPress

CENTER FOR HOLOCAUST STUDIES NEWSLETTER

client

MUSEUM OF JEWISH HERITAGE

business

MUSEUM

design firm

RIGELHAUPT DESIGN

art director

GAIL RIGELHAUPT

designers

GAIL RIGELHAUPT
HARRIS SILVER
LORRI SHUNDICH
JANETTE EUSEBIO

This magazine-like, two-color newsletter is severe without being too scholarly. And yet its design complements the seriousness of its mission.

pages 56-80, frequency Varies, quantity 10,000, software QuarkXPress, Aldus PageMaker

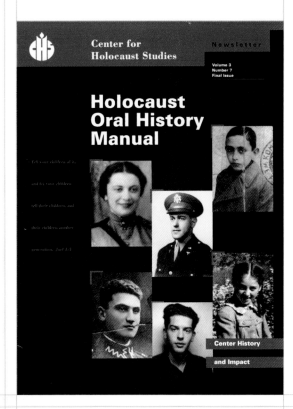

THE BARNES FOUNDATION

client

THE BARNES FOUNDATION

business

ART MUSEUM/SCHOOL

design firm

REV VISUAL

art director

MARJORIE GORMAN

designer

RICHARD B. CRESS

This four-color, six-page foldout is not inexpensive to produce, but neither does it go to excess. It remains true to the concept of the newsletter and uses color to attract readers in a competitive field.

pages 6, frequency Quarterly, quantity 5,000, software QuarkXPress

Cooper-Hewitt National Design Museum Smithsonian Institution

MAGAZINE Winter 1995

NATIONAL DESIGN MUSEUM MAGAZINE

client

NATIONAL DESIGN MUSEUM, SMITHSONIAN INSTITUTION

business

MUSEUM

design firm

DRENTTEL DOYLE PARTNERS

art director

STEPHEN DOYLE

designers

TOM KLUEPFEL
ROSEMARIE TURK
GARY TOOTH
RUTH DIENER
VANESSA ECKSTEIN

photographer

DENNIS COWLEY

Is it a book or a magazine?
This newsletter is in the size
of a book and the format of
a magazine. This programs
and information listing is
designed and edited with
short stories that do not
simply list, but promote the
lectures, exhibitions and
tours sponsored by the
museum.

pages 64, frequency
Quarterly, quantity 30,000

FRAMEWORKS

client

SAN JOSE MUSEUM OF ART

business

ART MUSEUM

design firm

PENTAGRAM

art director

KIT HINRICHS

designer

ANNE CULBERTSON

photographer

SAN JOSE MUSEUM OF ART

This large, four-color tabloid looks more like a smart magazine than a newsletter. The distinctive logo is framed by an almost full-page photograph, which in turn, is grounded by a bank of referal headlines.

pages 8, frequency Quarterly, quantity 7,500, software QuarkXPress

FRAMEWORKS   SAN JOSE MUSEUM OF ART

WINTER 1995

ANDY GOLDSWORTHY, "BREATH OF EARTH," RUNNYMEDE, CA, 1994

In This Issue: CALIFORNIA'S NATURAL RESOURCES ARE FEATURED IN THE EXHIBITION "ANDY GOLDSWORTHY: BREATH OF EARTH," **PAGE 3**   THE MUSEUM KICKS OFF THE FIFTH SEASON OF SAN JOSE JAZZ SOCIETY SUNDAY CONCERTS, **PAGE 5**   FIND OUT WHAT MAKES APPLE COMPUTER, INC. A MUSEUM STAR, **PAGE 7**   VISIT THE SAN JOSE MUSEUM OF ART'S BOOK AND GIFT SHOP IN ITS TWO NEW LOCATIONS, **PAGE 6**

Smithsonian Institution
Traveling Exhibition Service
Washington DC 20560
Number 35
Fall 1993

siteline

Meet Our Jazz Orchestra

"Night Life is cut out of a very luxurious, royal blue bolt of velvet. It sparkles with jewels, and it sparkles in tingling and tinkling tones," Duke Ellington once said, conjuring the glittery avenues where he and his orchestra performed in some of the world's great cities. As visitors to *Beyond Category: The Musical Genius of Duke Ellington* walk through theatrical settings that recreate these legendary environments, Ellington thrills them with his own account of one of the most fascinating lives of the twentieth century – from his boyhood days in Washington, D.C., to the bright lights of New York and eventually to the worldwide stage.

"*Beyond Category* has two levels of narration," explains Deborah Macanic, SITES project director for the exhibition. "Text panels present facts and information of historical importance, but in a second tier of narration – quotes presented throughout the exhibition – one can hear the voices of Duke Ellington, his family, musicians, and close associates, telling Duke's story in their own words."

Taking a cue from this highly successful new project, we've asked a few members of the ensemble behind *Beyond Category* to describe first-hand their encounters with Ellington – and their future plans to enliven the American scene with the richness of jazz history and sound.

Continued on page 4

A publicity shot of Ellington, emphasizing his elegant and graceful persona.

SITELINE
client
SMITHSONIAN INSTITUTION
business
MUSEUM
design firm
GRAFIK COMMUNICATIONS LTD.
designers
GREGG GLAVIANO
RICHARD HAMILTON
JUDY KIRPICH
photographer
MAURICE OF CHICAGO

This four-color tabloid printed on glossy stock is awash with a variety of images. The entire presentation has the authoritative air of a magazine, but, given blurbs and news bits definitely signal a newsletter.

pages 8, frequency Quarterly, quantity 15,000, software Aldus PageMaker

VIEW

c l i e n t

MUSEUM OF
CONTEMPORARY ART
SAN DIEGO

b u s i n e s s

ART MUSEUM

d e s i g n   f i r m s

PENTAGRAM/POWELL
STREET STUDIO

a r t   d i r e c t o r

KIT HINRICHS

d e s i g n e r

LINDA HINRICHS

p h o t o g r a p h e r

DAVID NASH

This two-color newsletter is
much more austere than the
San Francisco Museum of
Modern Art, Architecture &
Design Journals, but no less
visually exciting. The merci-
fully short articles are set
on a four-column grid, with
type set flush left, allowing
air into the format.

pages 14, frequency
Quarterly, quantity 7,000,
software QuarkXPress,
Microsoft Word

MUSEUM OF CONTEMPORARY ART SAN DIEGO

VIEW

JULY·AUGUST·SEPTEMBER·QUARTERLY NEWSLETTER 1994

EXHIBITIONS *David Nash: Voyages and Vessels
Nancy Rubins*: "Airplane Parts and Building, A Large Growth
for San Diego"· *inSITE94*: Anya Gallaccio·Yukinori Yanagi
Carlos Aguirre **EDUCATION** STREETsmART Update·
Lectures: David Nash·Robert Venturi·Denise Scott Brown
Ronald J.Onorato **SPECIAL EVENTS** Monte Carlo '94
Benefit Preview Performance: Spalding Gray in "Gray's Anatomy"
MUSEUM NEWS July 14: Groundbreaking in La Jolla

DAVID NASH, DETAIL OF "BLACK DOME", 1989 (2 PARTS: CANVAS DRAWING, CHARRED CHESTNUT), CHESTNUT AND CHARCOAL ON CANVAS, COLLECTION CAPEL RHIW

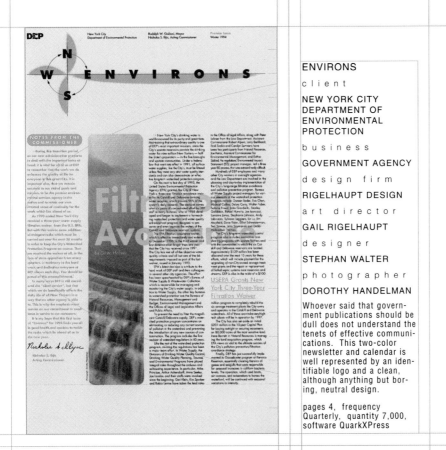

ENVIRONS

client

NEW YORK CITY DEPARTMENT OF ENVIRONMENTAL PROTECTION

business

GOVERNMENT AGENCY

design firm

RIGELHAUPT DESIGN

art director

GAIL RIGELHAUPT

designer

STEPHAN WALTER

photographer

DOROTHY HANDELMAN

Whoever said that government publications should be dull does not understand the tenets of effective communications. This two-color newsletter and calendar is well represented by an identifiable logo and a clean, although anything but boring, neutral design.

pages 4, frequency Quarterly, quantity 7,000, software QuarkXPress

FUSION

client

BELLAS ARTES INTERNATIONAL

business

ARTISTS' REPRESENTATIVES

design firm

POWELL STREET STUDIO

designer

LINDA HINRICHS

photographer

RICHARD WALKER

This photographically inspired design is a contemporary approach. The tabloid form allows for maximum impact of the represented artists' work and serves as both catalog and newsletter.

pages 8, frequency Varies, quantity 5,000, software QuarkXPress, Microsoft Word

AMMI QUARTERLY
GUIDE TO
EXHIBITIONS &
PROGRAMS

client

AMERICAN MUSEUM OF
THE MOVING IMAGE

business

MUSEUM

design firm

ALEXANDER ISLEY
DESIGN

art director

ALEXANDER ISLEY

designer

DAVID ALBERTSON

photographer

MUKY MUNKACSI

This lovely booklet is printed in two colors throughout.
The boxed logo on the cover
moves around each issue,
while inside the constantly
changing layouts are
designed with the subjects
in mind. Continued on
pages 76 and 77.

pages 20, frequency
Quarterly, quantity 10,000,
software QuarkXPress

Muky's New York:

Photographer to the Postwar Film Renaissance

Opens May 14, 1994

The motion picture industry in New York was revived in the 1950s, when talents like Marlon Brando, Sidney Lumet and Budd Schulberg defied the traditional Hollywood notion of what American movies should be.

Working with an innovative group of East Coast cinematographers, they pioneered a dramatic visual style which owed more to photojournalism than to glamour or advertising photography. The stylized realism of films like *The Fugitive Kind*, *Midnight Cowboy*, and *The Miracle Worker* became the hallmark of New York's film renaissance. And for 25 years most of it was documented by one man, a still photographer named Muky Munkacsi.

Like most of the great New York still cameramen, Muky is seldom included in histories

ON THE COVER: Paul Newman in THE HUSTLER. Photo by Muky.

**CLOCKWISE FROM TOP: STAGE STRUCK, THE FUGITIVE KIND, THE WORLD OF HENRY ORIENT.
OPPOSITE PAGE LEFT TO RIGHT: STILL OF THE NIGHT, Muky Munkacsi, 12 ANGRY MEN.**

of Hollywood glamour photography. The oversight is not surprising. Instead of shooting in portrait studios, Muky took his Hasselblads and Nikons out into the city streets, or shot his actors from the corners of sets built into cramped shooting stages in Brooklyn or the Bronx.

Muky's first film work was done in Hollywood, where for a time he had a portrait studio at Warner Bros. down the hall from George Hurrell. He quickly captured the look and feel of the typical Hollywood movie-star portrait, but his most interesting work was done on special assignment for the picture magazines. Here he could ignore convention and roam the soundstages with small-format cameras. *Citizen Kane* provided some memorable opportunities, but Muky was just not the Hollywood type, and he soon returned to New York.

Working as a commercial photographer in New York after World War II, Muky took advantage of the new opportunities offered by television, and for a time even had his own show. It was inevitable that the energy of that "live from New York" era would one day spill over onto the big screen, however, and in 1956 he joined director Sidney Lumet on the landmark production of *Twelve Angry Men*.

It was the first of eight features Muky would document for Lumet, and of a new era in East Coast production. The pair worked together on *The Fugitive Kind*, *The Group*, *Dog Day Afternoon*, and a host of others, testing a range of familiar genres and recasting them in a distinctly New York style. Muky's photos of Kim Novak, Candice Bergen, and Meryl Streep typify this look: direct, no tricks, completely professional. The photographer draws little attention to himself without turning his subjects into outsize caricatures favored by press agents and entertainment journalists.

This exhibition is the first museum retrospective ever of Muky's photography, and is made possible through the generous donation of nearly 1,000 images by Ronald A. and Randy P. Munkacsi.

Still photographers are seldom credited on screen, and to see the line "Photo by Muky" one usually has to track down a set of original prints. Until now that hasn't been very easy, but after 25 years of his documenting the work of others, the time has come to turn some light on the photographer himself.

Organized by Richard Koszarski, Head of Collections & Exhibitions.

MEET MUKY AT AMMI!
Saturday, May 14, 1:00 p.m.
Muky Munkacsi will be at the Museum to open *Muky's New York* at 1:00 p.m. on Saturday, May 14. Be here to greet the dean of New York's motion picture still photographers during this rare personal appearance.

"That fall of 1928 I went around with my little box camera taking pictures of every marquee that had my name in lights. From this period on, I was never again carefree. Before, I had been absolutely sure of myself in a brash and very young way. Now I began to study and observe myself. I was immersed with my own image on the screen... But I did have enough sense to know that I must work, and work hard. I kept setting the goal higher and higher."

—Joan Crawford

Willful, determined, single-minded. These virtues defined Joan Crawford: the woman, the roles she played, and the mythology that surrounded her. Crawford was one of Hollywood's most driven stars; working within the elaborate machinery of the studio system, she devoted her life and career to crafting, redefining, and shaping her own image.

Joan Crawford
April 2-May 15, 1994

Trained as a dancer, she started her screen career as a flapper, the essence of femininity. *Our Dancing Daughters*, her 1928 smash hit, has aptly been compared to *Saturday Night Fever* for its cultural impact: thousands of teenage girls used the film as a model for how to dress, wear their hair, and behave.

In the early 1930s, when she was at the pinnacle of her stardom, her archetypal role

Born Lucille LeSueur, Crawford was christened in a fan-magazine contest that offered $1,000 for the name that would best express her "energetic, ambitious, and typically American personality." Indeed, energy and ambition were the qualities that marked both the bright and the dark sides of the Crawford persona.

was the rags-to-riches working-class woman, mirroring her own highly publicized background as a small-town girl who used pluck and determination to become a star. Unlike Garbo or Dietrich,

April
May
June
1993

SAN FRANCISCO
MUSEUM OF MODERN
ART, ARCHITECTURE
& DESIGN JOURNAL

client

SAN FRANCISCO
MUSEUM OF MODERN
ART

business

ART MUSEUM

design firm

POWELL STREET
STUDIO

designer

LINDA HINRICHS

illustrators

MICHAEL CRONAN
MICHAEL MANWARING
MICHAEL VANDERBYL
GERALD REIS

photographer

JACK MCDONALD

pages 8-12, frequency
1-2/year, quantity 2,000-
10,000, software
QuarkXPress, Microsoft
Word

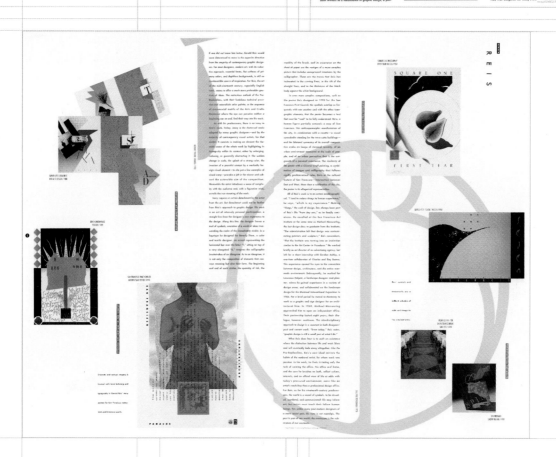

VOLUME III, NUMBER I ~ OCTOBER 1993

THE COLOR OF ELEMENTS
THE ARCHITECTURE OF MARK MACK

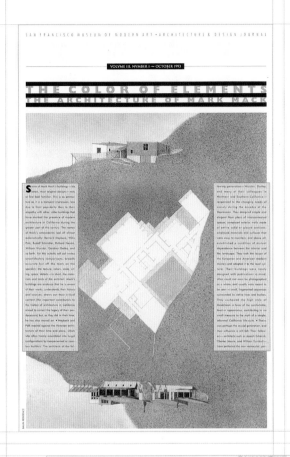

MACK RESIDENCE

SAN FRANCISCO MUSEUM OF MODERN ART, ARCHITECTURE & DESIGN JOURNAL

client

SAN FRANCISCO MUSEUM OF MODERN ART

business

ART MUSEUM

design firm

POWELL STREET STUDIO

designer

LINDA HINRICHS

illustrator

MARK MACK

photographer

RICHARD BARNES

This four-color tabloid is a feast for the eyes. In addition to an array of beautiful and imaginative typographic treatments, the illustrations are given a lavish full-page treatment.

pages 8-12, frequency 1-2/year, quantity 2,000-10,000, software QuarkXPress, Microsoft Word

> "California provides a gentle climate which allows architecture to be expressed as a metaphor of living in nature rather than in a mechanically conditioned environment. These climatic realities are the elemental building blocks of a program which contributes to the interdependence of architecture and environment in a site-specific relationship."

> "Trellis is a climatic mediator between nature and architecture. This informal outdoor structure brings the garden into the house and the house into the garden, extending the livable area of the domestic environment."

> "Privacy as a value remains respect in America, a puzzling issue for a country which is built on the constitutional values of individuality. I look to Mexican, Mediterranean and other cultural examples in which societal needs for privacy were balanced with the needs for public places."

> "Color is for me the virtue of optimism and codifies the architectural intention in a loosely defined and envisioned spectrum. I am trying to use color in a personal, coloured way—a non-dogmatic, casual use of color and elements that I associate with the California sensibility."

BCM CALENDAR

client

THE BROOKLYN
CHILDREN'S MUSEUM

business

MUSEUM

design firm

BCM GRAPHICS

art director/
designer

MARCELLO ARAVJO

illustrator

MARCELLO ARAVJO

This two-color, accordion-
fold newsletter is designed
to be read by children and
adults, and the graphics are
suitable for both. The use
of an off-white paper stock
gives the illusion that this is
printed in more than two
colors.

pages 2, frequency
Quarterly, quantity 10,000,
software QuarkXPress, Aldus
Freehand, Adobe Photoshop

ZOO VIEWS

client

SAN FRANCISCO
ZOOLOGICAL SOCIETY

business

ZOO

design firm

COLEMAN SOUTER
DESIGN

art director

MARK COLEMAN

designers

KARYN NELSON
ERIK WATTS

photographer

STEVEN UNDERWOOD
PHOTOGRAPHY

This four-color tabloid is as
exciting as the attractions at
the zoo. In fact, for the
couch potato, it brings these
attractions vividly to life.
With its strong cover image
(usually of an animal) and
bold, lively feature spreads,
a wealth of useful information is graphically conveyed.

pages 12, frequency
Bimonthly, quantity 10,000

> half empty <

R E S E R V E

7

FEDERAL
RESERVE
BANK
OF CHICAGO

SECOND
QUARTER
1993

< half full >

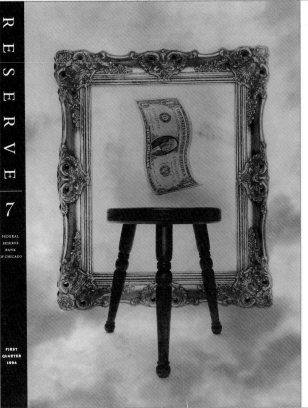

RESERVE 7

client

FEDERAL RESERVE
BANK OF CHICAGO

business

BANK

design firm

CONCRETE

designers

JILLY SIMONS
DAVID ROBSON

illustrator

GERALD BUSTAMANTE
(bottom right)

R E S E R V E

7

FEDERAL
RESERVE
BANK
OF CHICAGO

FIRST
QUARTER
1994

p h o t o g r a p h e r s

DANIEL ARSENAULT
(top left)

WILLIAM VALICENTI
(top right)

PETER ROSENBAUM
(bottom left)

Some newsletters are designed to approximate annual reports. This glossy, full-color quarterly looks, feels, and reads like one. Only its purpose is to provide news and information on a more frequent basis.

pages 20, frequency Quarterly, quantity 4,500, software QuarkXPress

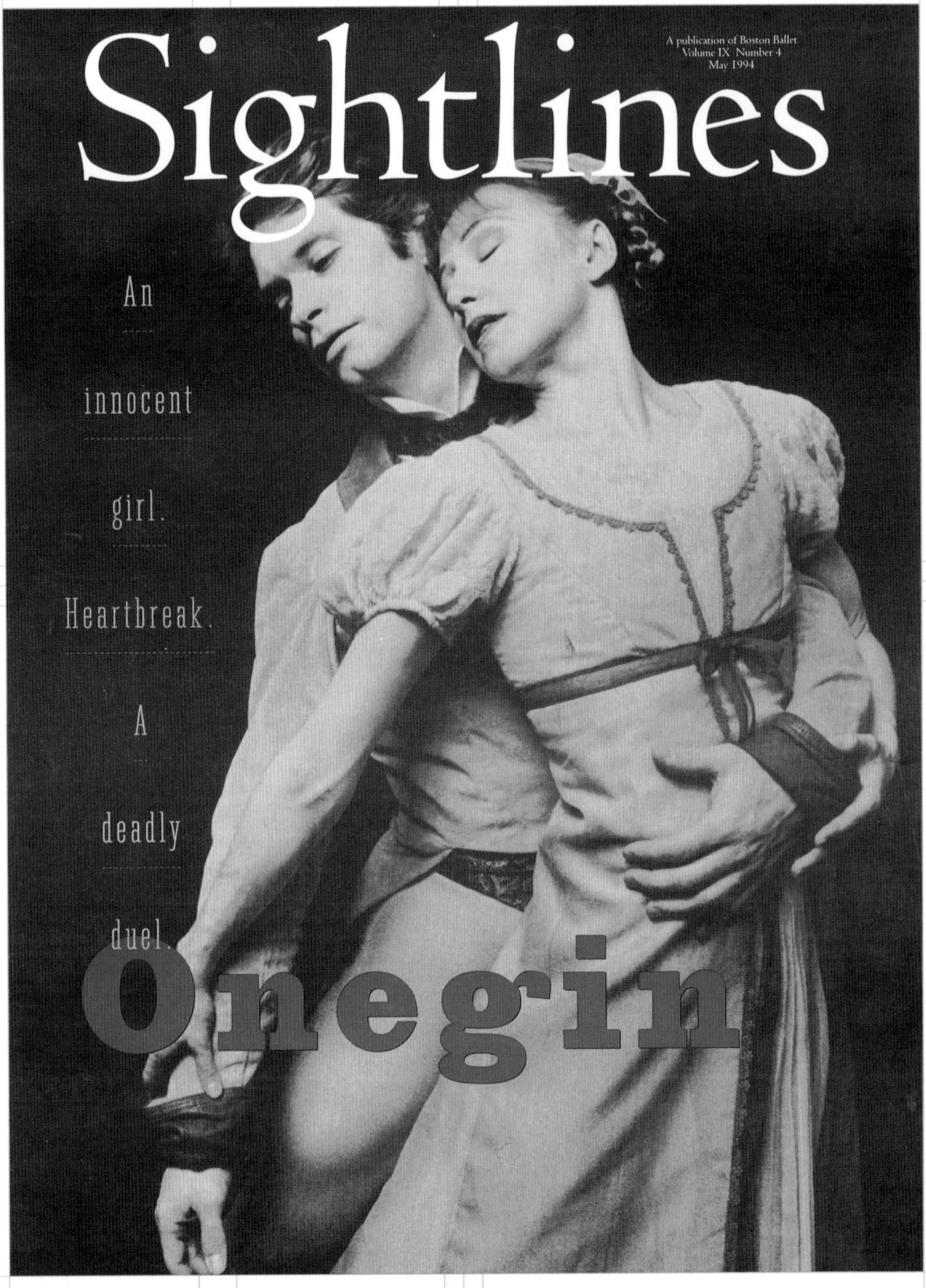

Sightlines

A publication of Boston Ballet
Volume IX Number 4
May 1994

An

innocent

girl.

Heartbreak.

A

deadly

duel.

Onegin

SITELINES

client
BOSTON BALLET

business
BALLET COMPANY

design firm
RONN CAMPISI DESIGN

designer
RONN CAMPISI

photographer
JERRY BERNDT

With only two colors—and a generous use of duotones—this newsletter approximates the look of the so-called culture-tabs. Newsier stories, designed in a low-key manner, sandwich two or more striking feature spreads where the type and image explode off the page.

pages 12, frequency Quarterly, quantity 15,000, software QuarkXPress

performance preview

Fiery

Dancing and

Drama

Steeped in

the Passion

of the

Russian

People

A Boston Ballet
Premiere
Production

ABOVE: DEVON CARNEY AND CLAUDIA ALFIERI AS THE ILL-FATED ONEGIN AND TATIANA. LEFT: PATRICK ARMAND AND NATASHA AKHMAROVA AS YOUNG LOVERS LENSKY AND OLGA. BELOW: PATRICK ARMAND AND TRINIDAD SEVILLANO PERFORM A SCENE FROM ONEGIN.

TO UNDERSTAND AND ENJOY John Cranko's masterpiece, *Onegin*, one needs only show up at the theater, sit back, and watch the action unfold. Although the history and story of *Onegin* are rich in detail and drama, Cranko's choreography truly tells a story through dance — not through mime or program notes — and the story to be told during *Onegin* far surpasses any plot of a modern day soap opera or Gothic romance. *Onegin* is a passionate, sometimes violent, and downright juicy love story. Each character is richly developed. The sets and costumes conjure up another time, another place. The Tchaikovsky music, arranged and orchestrated by Kurt-Heinz Stolze, never fails in setting just the right mood. And the dancing is some of the most challenging, beautiful, and dramatic in the 20th century repertoire. ¶ The great choreographer John Cranko enjoyed a remarkably productive and successful career, particularly with the Stuttgart Ballet which he directed from 1961 until his tragic, unexpected death in 1973 aboard an airplane *en route* from New York to Germany. He mounted countless ballet productions on a grand scale, including *Romeo and Juliet*, *The Taming of the Shrew* and, of course, *Onegin* which he created for Stuttgart Ballet in 1965. Boston Ballet will be the first American ballet company to perform this astounding work which is presented in three acts and six scenes.

Boston Ballet performs John Cranko's glorious, three-act ballet, Onegin, May 5 - 15 at The Wang Center.

Sightlines Boston Ballet May 1994 **7**

INOVA HEALTHSOURCE

INOVA HEALTHSOURCE

INOVA HEALTHSOURCE

INOVA HEALTHSOURCE

AIDS

AIDS is the final stage of disease caused by the human immunodeficiency virus (HIV) and usually takes many years to develop. In Northern Virginia, over 1200 people have AIDS and thousands more are infected with HIV. Although they may look and feel healthy, infected people can spread the virus to others through risky behavior.

AIDS is the 5th leading cause of death among women of childbearing age in the U.S.

An HIV-infected woman has a 30% chance of passing the virus to her fetus during pregnancy.

The Centers for Disease Control estimate that over one million people are infected with HIV in the U.S.

By 2000, there will be an equal number of infected men and women worldwide.

By 1995, the cumulative cost of caring for HIV-infected people in the U.S. will top $15 billion.

In the past six years, the number of HIV-infected teenagers has doubled every 14 months.

Assessing Risk

Most people get HIV by sharing needles or having unprotected sex with someone who already has the virus.

Your risk of contracting HIV is greatest if:
· you have engaged in unprotected, intimate sexual contact with one or more partners over the last 12-15 years
· you have shared needles while using injectable drugs over the last 12-15 years
· you had a blood transfusion between 1977 and 1985, before the blood supply was screened for HIV.

If you have been involved in a monogamous relationship for the last 12-15 years, never shared needles, or never had a blood transfusion, you are at very low risk for HIV infection.

If you think you are at risk, or for more help or information, call one of the numbers listed below.

Reducing Risk

There are basic precautions people can take to reduce or eliminate their risk of being infected with HIV. Abstaining from sex or, if sexually active, always using latex condoms, can help protect people from contracting HIV. Using injectable drugs only under a doctor's care, and never sharing needles with anyone, will also reduce the risk of HIV infection.

People cannot "catch" HIV like the cold or flu. The virus dies quickly outside the body and is not spread through shaking hands, coughing, hugging or from swimming pools or toilet seats.

Inova HIV Services

The Office of HIV Services was established in 1988 to lead Inova's efforts to respond to the AIDS epidemic. The office includes the HIV Center, which provides and coordinates a continuum of medical and personal services to those with HIV or AIDS, and the Northern Virginia HIV Resource & Consultation Center, which educates and trains the healthcare workers who care for HIV-infected patients.

| *For more information about AIDS and HIV contact:* | Inova Office of HIV Services 703-204-3780 or toll-free from anywhere in Virginia 1-800-828-4927 | Virginia AIDS Information Hotline 1-800-533-4148 | National AIDS Information Hotline 1-800-432-AIDS in Spanish 1-800-344-7432 | *Inova Health System Hospitals:* | · Fairfax Hospital · Fair Oaks Hospital · Mount Vernon Hospital |

INOVA HEALTH SYSTEM

INOVA HEALTHSOURCE

client
INOVA HEALTH SYSTEM

business
HEALTH CARE

design firm
PICTOGRAM STUDIO

art director
STEPHANIE HOOTON

designers
STEPHANIE HOOTON
HIEN NGUYEN

illustrator
HIEN NGUYEN

With limited means this is a most effective newsletter. One long and narrow trifold suggests a larger publication. One fold of each issue is a "cover" printed in a bright flat color that changes with each edition.

pages 1, frequency Quarterly, quantity 5,000, typography Photographic Typesetting

INOVA OUTLOOK

client

INOVA HEALTH SYSTEM

business

HEALTH CARE

design firm

PICTOGRAM STUDIO

art director

STEPHANIE HOOTON

designers

STEPHANIE HOOTON
HIEN NGUYEN

photographer

CLAUDIO VAZQUEZ

The cover of this three-color
tabloid newsletter always
has a photograph that illustrates the single cover story.
Inside contents are signified
by different logos.

pages 4, frequency
Quarterly, quantity 75,000,
typography Photographic
Typesetting

Issue 4
Midwinter 1993

Health news
and information
from
Inova Health
System

A COMMUNITY HEALTH RESOURCE

Inova*Outlook*

Measuring Progress, Meeting Needs

Keeping in close touch with community health needs is a critical
component of Inova Health System's
commitment to provide the highest
quality healthcare for Northern
Virginians. Inova recently conducted
a pioneering, comprehensive study
of the community's health status.
The results will be used to develop
and enhance community programs
and services and will be shared
with others to generate potential
collaborative projects.

Inova interviewed members of
different ethnic groups, community
leaders, Medicaid recipients, those
with no health insurance and those
fortunate enough to be insured. The
findings provide a broad assessment
of the community's general health,
as well as its principle health concerns
and needs.

The good news is that Northern
Virginians are healthier than
the average Virginian and American.
Heart disease and cancer are the
greatest health concerns, although
the study noted that heart disease
death rates have declined here over
the last five years. Nevertheless,
Northern Virginia still has a long way
to go to meet the goals in the U.S.
Department of Health and Human
Services' document *Healthy People
2000* for heart disease and cancer
mortality rates. (For study findings,
see inside page.)

AIDS is also of great concern locally.
The number of new AIDS cases has
grown dramatically in our region
over the last 10 years and residents
believe more AIDS education,
prevention and treatment services
are needed.

Generally, Northern Virginians are
satisfied with their healthcare services.

However, there is universal concern
about rising health and insurance
costs and the growing number of
uninsured. Many people cited the
need for more clinics for low-income
residents, more children's health
services, and more drug and alcohol
treatment programs.

Certain segments of the population—
Hispanics, African Americans,
Asians and those on Medicaid or
without health insurance—feel their
health needs have not been met as
well as others. Asians and Hispanics,
the two fastest growing populations
in Northern Virginia, require more
bilingual health services.

This comprehensive study will help
Inova to continue its leadership role
as the community's premier healthcare provider, while working to
control costs, foster access and reach
out to those with the greatest need.

INOVA
HEALTH SYSTEM

CANCER
PERSPECTIVES

client

THE CLEVELAND CLINIC
FOUNDATION

business

HOSPITAL/CLINIC

design firm

FELDMAN DESIGN

art director/
designer

JAMIE FELDMAN

illustrator

CATHIE BLECK

White space is generously
used in this two-color
newsletter. Every cover is
differently illustrated in a
conceptual, editorial
manner.

pages 4, frequency
Quarterly, quantity 5,000,
software QuarkXPress

CANCER
PERSPECTIVES

VOLUME 1 | ISSUE 1

genetics

Dear Friends:
On behalf of the Cleveland Clinic Cancer
Center, welcome to the first edition of
our newsletter, Cancer Perspectives.
It is our goal to bring you timely and
relevant information concerning
new developments in the
prevention, diagnosis and treatment of
cancer that may be important to you,
a family member or a friend.
We will include dates of our regularly
scheduled cancer screening programs as
well as dates of our upcoming, free public
seminars, Health Talks, that
are related to cancer topics.
Because of all of the recent attention
in the media about the breakthroughs in
gene research related to cancers that lead
to run in families, we have devoted this
issue of our newsletter to the advance-
ments that have occurred in how forms of
hereditary cancer, colorectal and breast.
We hope our publication will serve as a
two-way communication channel,
so please send us your comments,
questions and suggestions.
Sincerely,
Maurie Markman, M.D.
Director, Cancer Center

CLOSING IN ON CANCER'S ORIGIN | Unraveling the intricate events that turn a
normal cell into a cancerous one continue to perplex scientists. But advances made
by cancer biologists around the country are shedding new light on this complex
disease. Their foundation of knowledge is built on a discovery that scientists made
more than 30 years ago when they concluded that cells can become cancerous
when their genetic machinery suffers a breakdown. The culprit of that breakdown
may be traced to diet, environmental poisons, defective inherited genes, unknown
factors or a combination of all of these. Once the breakdown occurs, the gene's
normal function of controlling or regulating cell growth is lost, and the ground-
work is laid for cancer. Regardless of the cause, the common pathway to cancer
involves cell damage. | In their studies of cancer cells, scientists have found
mutated genes at nearly every step of the way, from the   *continued on page 2*

continued on page 2

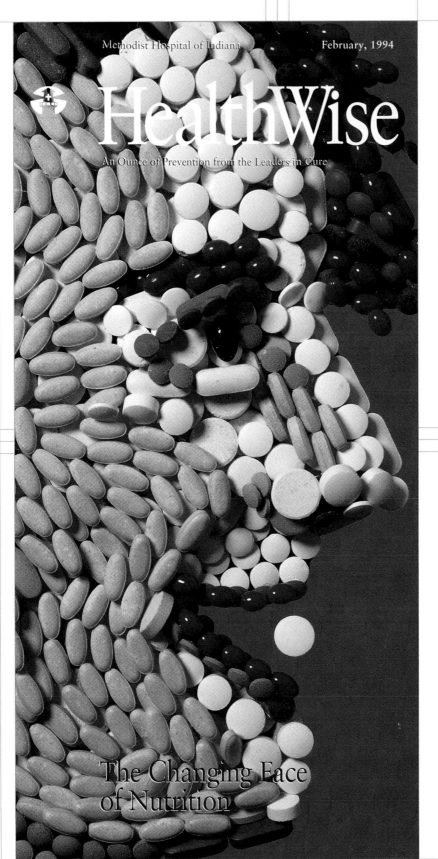

Methodist Hospital of Indiana

February, 1994

HealthWise

An Ounce of Prevention from the Leaders in Cure

The Changing Face
of Nutrition

HEALTHWISE

client

**METHODIST HOSPITAL
OF INDIANA**

business

HEALTH CARE

design firm

ESSEX TWO

art director

JOSEPH ESSEX

designers

**NANCY ESSEX
JOSEPH ESSEX**

illustrator

PAUL DOLAN

The four-color illustrated
cover suggests a magazine;
indeed it is a saddle-stitched
booklet with color used
throughout, not unlike an
annual report. But it is
intended to serve the same
function as a more tightly
budgeted newsletter.

pages 24, frequency
Quarterly, quantity 15,000,
software QuarkXPress

INITIATIVES

client

UNITED WAY OF NEW
YORK CITY

business

SOCIAL SERVICES

design firm

CALFO/ARON, INC.

designers

MICHAEL ARON
JASON CALFO

illustrators

JOHN HOWARD
(top left)

CATHIE BLECK
(bottom left)

RANDY LYHUS
(top right)

PHILIPPE LARDY
(bottom right)

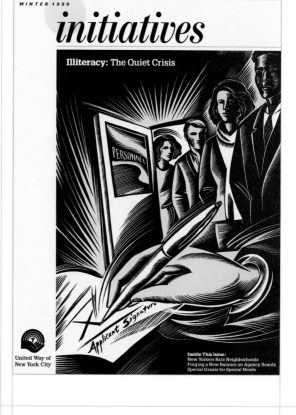

SPRING/SUMMER 1992

initiatives

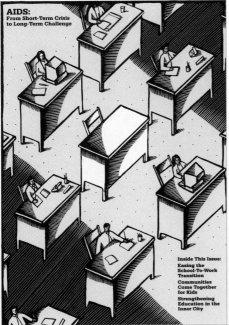

AIDS:
From Short-Term Crisis
to Long-Term Challenge

Inside This Issue:
Easing the
School-To-Work
Transition
Communities
Come Together
for Kids
Strengthening
Education in the
Inner City

United Way of
New York City

SUMMER 1990

initiatives

Confronting
New York City's
Problems:

**Setting A
Human Service
Agenda for
the 90's**

Inside This Issue:
Tackling Race Relations
New Federations Serve Growing Immigrant Groups
Impact: Youth Unemployment

United Way of
New York City

Charitable organizations
have to compete in a huge
arena that necessitates eye-
catching, though not over-
done, graphics. This two-
color newsletter succeeds at
capturing the reader's attention. The single front page
story and additional pull-
quotes or contents
announcements on the front
page are deftly
handled.

pages 8, frequency
Quarterly, quantity 10,000,
software QuarkXPress

SAFETY NET

client

COALITION FOR THE
HOMELESS

business

HOMELESS ADVOCACY

design firm

STUDIO MORRIS

art director

JEFF MORRIS

designers

KAORU SATO
JEFF MORRIS

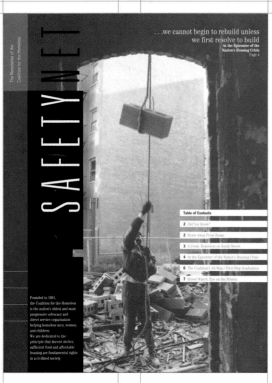

An example of low-budget design, this two-color quarterly introduces its difficult subject with a well-designed photographic cover, set against a memorable masthead. The cover is usually a posterlike crop of a homeless person or environment, while the interior is handsome no-frills design.

pages 8, frequency Quarterly, quantity 10,000, software QuarkXPress, Adobe Photoshop

The Coalition for the Homeless
The Shelter Newsletter
Volume One, Number One
September 1994
Free

What's Going On?

VERNELL ROBINSON AND JENIFER MITAS

An active Client Advisory Board ensures the quality of shelter resident's lives when the Department of Homeless Services won't.

Strong Client Advisory Boards work with shelter staff to curb abuse and negligence. But most shelters don't have a Board. Shelter organizer, Vernell Robinson sums it up, "The New York City shelter system suffers from a severe lack of staff support and client participation."

Some shelter residents report that they are afraid to speak out about problems they want addressed. They don't want to be pinpointed as troublemakers to be punitively transferred or further picked on by angry staff members. The same crimes continue to be committed against residents but there's no client police body (CAB) to blow the whistle. Meanwhile...the food is rotten, the washing machines are broken, client donations are stolen and staff is abusive.

If you're someone who believes in the merits of self-government and action, we encourage you to come to the New York City Client Advisory Group meetings where you'll meet other Client Advisory Board members.

For information about visiting other shelters, as an organizer, contact Vernell Robinson at the Coalition for the Homeless, (212) 964-5900, extension 21. ●

Midtown Shelter Resident Uncovers Thieving Shelter Staff

ANONYMOUS

A midtown, shelter resident, who chooses to remain anonymous, repeatedly sees evening staff members leave the facility with garbage bags full of food- frozen dinners, cartons of milk, juice cups, fruit cups, bread and butter. Security guards open the refrigerators where resident meals are kept and snack on the job. Donations of clothing that come in through the facility basement are dragged upstairs by security guards, in to the staff room, where they take what they want and leave the leftovers for the residents. As she recounts these stories, the witness fumes, "There are no firm hands here. The staff steal and never get caught."

She reports the thievery to her caseworker and the shelter director, who asked her to speak at the next Client Advisory Board meeting. Although the director 'listened,' nothing else was done to insure that the staff stopped. The witness would like to see a work program started for residents, so that

they could take part in the upkeep of their own facility. She doesn't think that residents would steal food or donations or keep the best for themselves. The night staff are the main culprits- no one is around to watch them.

After she reported the incidents to the CAB, she got nervous. She said, "I see too much." She's afraid for her safety - if the staff knew that she watched them they might take action to make sure she kept quiet.

She asks, "Why don't they get rid of lazy guards who polish their nails and talk on the phone?" Wherever you go, guards stand up- at the airport, jewelry store, Macy's, the hospital. Here, they sit and if someone falls and calls for help, they ignore her." She remembers a time when an elderly friend's locker fell on top of her and the guard just sat there, bug-eyed. "They should run like hell with concern." So, why isn't DHS running like hell with concern about thieving, lazy shelter staff? ●

Join StreetWatch

Help or Harm?

JAMES KIZER GRAY

My name is James Kizer Gray. I am a prophet and my destiny is to become successful and famous. I used to be homeless, sleeping in cardboard boxes, hanging out on the streets. When I found out about the Grand Central Partnership's (GCP), "job training program," I thought, "Yeah, I'm graduating from homelessness to working for the homeless." First, I worked as a volunteer for four months. Later, I became a staff member for fifty dollars a week. My work was considered so outstanding, that they put me in charge of the kitchen at night and later promoted me to the outreach program. I went to banks and told homeless people they couldn't sleep in the area. All the Partnership ever did for homeless people was give them a sandwich and a chair to sleep in.

The Partnership came up with the idea of using the homeless to get to the homeless. They got people off the streets, into jails, hospitals or into the Partnership's waiting room. The Partnership called themselves a job training program but they never educated me or anyone else- they didn't give me a skill or help me get into permanent housing. They just showed me how to be a strong arm for the Partnership and how to sleep upright in a folding chair.

The Partnership has made the fight to eradicate homeless-ness a money-making superficial course, instead of a human-caring course.

Sometimes we chased people from the choice spots, so that later my group and I could go sleep there. The Partnership told us to focus on certain areas that they were paid by local businesses to keep "clean" (free of homeless people). Businesses who didn't pay, "paid" when we drove homeless people to their doorsteps. We, as "outreach workers" were paid forty to fifty dollars a week.

The Partnership has kissed media butt lately and they've been presented as an innovative social service organization, using the "homeless to help the homeless." Actually, they use the homeless to harm the homeless, shuffling them around the city and offering good-for-nothing services with money that is meant to really help homeless people. Before you can say that a bed is a good bed, you have to sleep in it. ●

"Company Union"

Lisa Daugaard

The last newsletter discussed how the Department of Homeless Services (DHS), has tried to start new "Client Advisory Committees" (CAC), similar in many ways to the existing Client Advisory Boards but with one crucial difference: unlike the current CAB's, DHS would have almost complete control over which clients would serve on the CAC's and what issues the committees could discuss. DHS has proposed that shelter directors approve the agenda for CAC meetings in advance.

It is no coincidence that DHS has been trying to reduce the independence of the existing CAB's. The CAB structure has gotten more and more solid in most shelters in the last year, following Camp La Guardia's stellar example. Through sustained organizing efforts by some former shelter residents, and a long-term commitment by the Coalition for the Homeless to support CABs, they have been established at various shelters through the city. In CAB, residents can most effectively advocate for themselves. In the past year, CABs have hit hard, exposing the rotten shelter food racket, and protesting the Mayor's new plan to relegate out any shelter resident who fails to comply with a "service contract." In response, DHS is trying to co-opt the CABs. In so doing, they are following the famous "company union" model.

The "company union" is one of the oldest tricks in the book for employers whose workers start organizing effectively. Rather than recognize the employees' own union, the company forms its own "employee involvement committee," which deals with the same issues as the real union, with just one little difference: management appoints committee members, the terms under which they serve, and sets the limits of their authority. The company always has the final word, and can set aside the recommendations of the employee involvement if they become too threatening to the powers that be. The beauty of the company union for management is that it confuses the workers about how best to have their concerns heard and addressed. On the surface, it can seem as though working with management's own committee would be more effective than joining an oppositional union that management won't talk to. But labor movement history proves that company unions get employees nowhere. *For that reason, the National Labor Relations Act that made company unions illegal, was passed in 1930.*

Continued

X

client

COALITION FOR THE HOMELESS

business

HOMELESS ADVOCACY

design firm

VICTORE DESIGN WORKS

art director/ designer

JAMES VICTORE

illustrator

JAMES VICTORE

Here is the most no-frills newsletter of all: one sheet of newsprint photocopied on both sides (called a broadsheet). This is design at its minimalist. Nevertheless, the layout is not ad hoc but carefully composed for maximum impact.

pages 1, frequency Quarterly, quantity 5,000, software QuarkXPress

SCENE

client

THE CENTER FOR CHILDREN AND FAMILIES

business

SOCIAL SERVICES

design firm

RIGELHAUPT DESIGN

art director

GAIL RIGELHAUPT

designers

GAIL RIGELHAUPT
JANETTE EUSEBIO

The six-page foldout of this newsletter is one way to cut down on printing and paper costs. It also feels more immediate than other newsletters, particularly given its distorted type-writer-type logo, an overused but here, effective cliché.

pages 6, frequency Quarterly, quantity 5,000, software QuarkXPress, Adobe Photoshop

INFOLINES

client

AID ATLANTA

business

AIDS SERVICE ORGANIZATION

design firm

WAGES DESIGN

designers

RORY MYERS
MIKE NELSON

photographers

SUSAN HICKSON
ARRINGTON HENDLEY
KARA DOME

This startling two-color cover printed on off-white stock showcases various typographic conceits, including a logo that looks as if it's "hot off the press."

pages 6, frequency Monthly, quantity 9,000

THE CENTER FOR CHILDREN + FAMILIES, INC.

161-20 89th Avenue
Jamaica, New York 11432
718. 526.0722

NON-PROFIT ORG.
U.S. POSTAGE
PAID
PERMIT NO. 8
JAMAICA, NY

Join us in the Southeastern United States' largest AIDS fundraiser!

AIDS WALK ATLANTA

SUNDAY • OCT 16 • 1994

Photo by Susan Hoxon

Walkathon expects another record-breaking year

Registration cards and calls pour into the AIDS Walk Atlanta office as staff and volunteers brace themselves for a record breaking turnout on Sunday, October 16, 1994. A direct mail invitation from Cindy Crawford and Richard Gere, a televised Public Service Announcement featuring film star Matthew Broderick, 6,000 point of purchase stands dispersed throughout Atlanta and neighboring cities, and a volunteer phone bank have all helped recruitment figures out-pace the 1993 campaign. Last year walkers turned in $1,013,000.

The event begins at 1:00 p.m. at Piedmont Park when walkers turn in the pledges they have collected. At 1:30, an opening ceremony will feature celebrities, entertainers, and community leaders. The ten kilometer walk begins at

Photo by Arrington Hendley

2:00 p.m. and follows a route through the neighborhoods surrounding the park.

Participants take on the challenge of raising funds for the Walk by asking friends, family members, co-workers, and neighbors to sponsor them for each kilometer walked. Proceeds benefit AID Atlanta, Project Open Hand, and a variety of other outstanding AIDS Service

Organizations in Atlanta, providing direct services for men, women and children living with HIV disease.

After the opening ceremony, AIDS Walk Atlanta participants will exit Piedmont Park and walk the ten kilometer route through the picturesque Ansley Park area. Most walkers will complete the route in two hours then return to Piedmont Park for refreshments and a

post walk concert that will include live performances and an announcement of the total funds raised by the event.

Walkers who turn in $100 or more will be sent an official AIDS Walk Atlanta T-shirt, featuring the full color AIDS Walk graphic.

Sponsors for this year's Walk include: Cabbage Patch Kids, John Wieland Homes, NationsBank, Sprint, WSB-TV Family2Family, and Southern Voice.

Over one thousand volunteers are required on the day of the Event to help produce the AIDS Walk. Many volunteers raise funds in addition to helping make the day run smoothly.

To register to walk or volunteer for the AIDS Walk, call 876-WALK. Those interested in forming teams can receive specially coded registration kits for their company or group.

Photo by Kara Dome

Photo by Kara Dome

INFO.LINES (1994)

Info.lines is a quarterly publication of AID Atlanta. We hope you enjoy reading Info.lines and would like to hear any comments or suggestions. A special THANKS to Mike Nelson for his generous efforts in creating

AID Atlanta ©

by AID Atlanta, Inc.

the publication AID Atlanta, Inc. is a non-profit corporation providing human services to people affected by HIV/AIDS and education to the public about the causes, prevention, and treatment of HIV infection.

section II

mix matters

MTV Networks' Diversity Newsletter

issue #6

Stranger in a Strange Land

WESTERN AND EASTERN HEMISPHERES.

NORTHERN AND SOUTHERN HEMISPHERES

Editorial

Sometimes one hasn't far to go to feel like a stranger in a strange land. The next town, city or neighborhood might be a very different experience. I grew up in the New York / Connecticut area and then (with encouragement from my parents) chose a southern college for a change of scene. It was the middle of the Eisenhower years, and I hadn't been far from home before.

Virginia was another world to me, and I was apprehensive, but the distance was too far to travel home on weekends, so I coped. For the first time in my life I was in a minority position - a Yankee and a Catholic all at once! Before too long I found other "strangers" and a good sense of myself, and the land was no longer strange. And I learned a lot about myself and others.

To make a change easier: prepare yourself before you go; investigate the culture, read . . .

Where would many of us be if we hadn't met a stranger or visited a strange land? Would we be at **MTV NETWORKS**? Would we be who we are? ✈

MIX MATTERS #6

client

MTV NETWORKS

business

CABLE TELEVISION

design firm

ERIC BAKER DESIGN
ASSOCIATES

art director

ERIC BAKER

designer

KAI ZIMMERMANN

Each issue of this important
workers' diversity newsletter
is different than the last. In
each, the subject dictates
the design. Here the map
suggests the geographic and
cultural diversity of the
MTV staff.

pages Foldout, frequency
Bimonthly, quantity 2,800,
software Adobe Illustrator

Special
MIXMASTERS Programs

In January Dr. Betty Shabazz spoke to us regarding diversity and answered many questions regarding racism and its ramifications. She emphasized the importance of not making assumptions with a story of a child in her children's school whose teacher thought he had family problems because his mother dressed up and went out all night. When the child's mother came to school for a conference she was wearing a nurse's uniform. Dr. Shabazz spoke briefly about her wanting to withdraw from life after her husband's assassination. She realized that she could not and has since become a role model for women everywhere.

In the 1992 MTVN survey it was found that only 19% of the Company participated in religious services on a regu-

lar basis. So, it was interesting to listen to and question the speakers presented by MIXMASTERS on May 11th in the Lodge. The speakers represented alternatives to organized religion as many of us know it.

Dr. Frank Kaufman from Pace University's Department of Religion spoke about religious diversity and world peace. Dr. Kaufman is Director of the Inter-Religious Federation for World Peace. While our government was cautioning North Korea not to develop nuclear arms, Dr. Kaufman's group was in North Korea establishing a dialogue with its leader.

Otter Zell, Founder, Church of All Worlds - a religion "dedicated to the celebration of Life, the maximal actualization of Human potential, and the realization of

ultimate individual freedom and personal responsibility in harmonious eco-psychic relationship with the total biosphere of Holy Mother Earth" spoke about religion and environmental issues. He expressed great hope for the world because women are gaining power, and, he feels, that is very important to the preservation of culture.

Joy Williams, liaison for the Church of All Worlds over the Internet, spoke about her experiences engaging in theological discussions over the computer "Info Superhighway" with people from all walks of religious orientation.

And - in June - we celebrated Gay Pride Month with a program on the 22nd; Breaking Stereotypes. With our own Robert Locke moderating we listened to Robbie Browne who was a swimmer in the Gay Games and who works for a major New York real estate firm. Robbie spoke about the games (straight people played too!) and about his life in New York City as a gay man. Paula Ettelbrick - attorney, activist, civil rights advocate and public policy director - shared her life experiences as a Lesbian in a straight

world - a world that was very lonely as she was growing up. All of us at the program realized that in order to respect someone, one first had to get to know the person.

MIXMASTERS hopes that those of you who did not attend were watching on Channel 3 and that you'll be able to attend these programs in the future or borrow the video from Lisa Lugtu x8911. The next program will be in September of this year.

MIXMASTERS, through programs and the newsletter MIXMATTERS, intends to present as many diversity issues as possible, in the best ways possible. Whatever we do is not meant to offend any individual or any group. If we provoke you, we want to know. We want to hear your views!

You can reach us via e-mail, interoffice, and/or drop a note into the Dialog Box. (There is one on each floor and in each region.) For publication of your views, or of diversity information you wish to share, please send a disk to Jeanne Cassidy, Concourse, 1515 Broadway. ⊬

MIX MATTERS #7

client

MTV NETWORKS

business

CABLE TELEVISION

design firm

ERIC BAKER DESIGN
ASSOCIATES

art director

ERIC BAKER

designer

MATHIEU ARAUD

This notepad format is a
rather self-conscious design
trick, but it has considerable
charm. Moreover, it is perfectly in sync with MTV's
overall aesthetic.

pages Notepad, frequency
Bimonthly, quantity 2,800,
software Adobe Illustrator

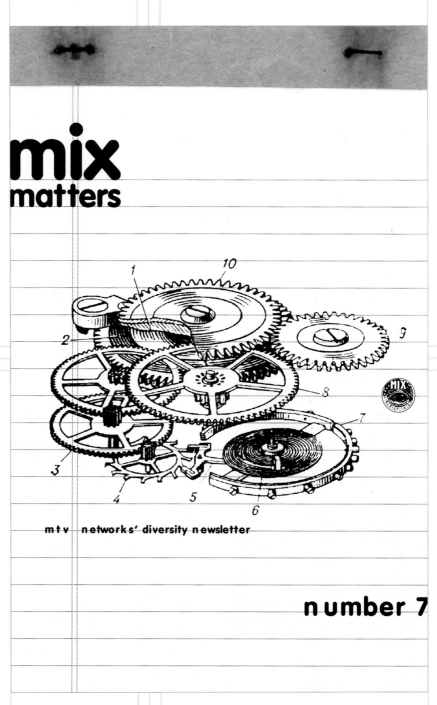

mix
matters

m t v n etwork s' diversity n ewsletter

n umber 7

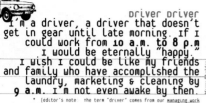

Driver Driver

I'm a driver, a driver that doesn't get in gear until late morning. If I could work from **10 a.m. to 8 p.m** I would be eternally "happy." I wish I could be like my friends and family who have accomplished the laundry, marketing & cleaning by **9 a.m.** I'm not even awake by then.

Kerry Sheldon

* (editor's note the term "driver" comes from our managing work relationships seminar, available through corporate training and development)

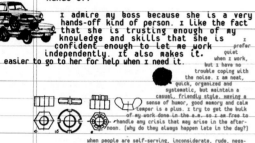

hands-off

I admire my boss because she is a very hands-off kind of person. I like the fact that she is trusting enough of my knowledge and skills that she is confident enough to let me work independently. It also makes it. easier to go to her for help when I need it.

I prefer quiet when I work, but I have no trouble coping with the noise. I am neat, quick, organized and systematic, but maintain a casual, friendly style. Having a sense of humor, good memory and calm temper is a plus. I try to get the bulk of my work done in the a.m. so I am free to handle any crisis that may arise in the afternoon. (why do they always happen late in the day?)

When people are self-serving, inconsiderate, rude, negative or lazy, nobody benefits, and it is actually very destructive when people are supposed to be working as a team. I admire people who are true to themselves, down-to-earth, honest, straightforward, sincere and positive in attitude. These people are success in my eyes whether their position is that of a mail clerk or ceo of the company.

working on the weekends

I wish everyday could be as productive as working on the weekends! I can do about **3 days** worth of "weekday" work on the weekends because the phone's not ringing and no one is around asking questions, etc.

I also love a good sense of humor- without it, we're doomed!

Shari Hoover

Diane Cassara

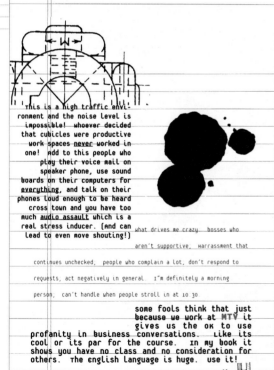

This is a high traffic environment and the noise level is impossible! whoever decided that cubicles were productive work spaces never worked in one! Add to this people who play their voice mail on speaker phone, use sound boards on their computers for everything, and talk on their phones loud enough to be heard cross town and you have too much audio assault which is a real stress inducer. (And can lead to even more shouting!)

what drives me crazy bosses who aren't supportive, harrassment that continues unchecked, people who complain a lot, don't respond to requests, act negatively in general. I'm definitely a morning person, can't handle when people stroll in at 10:30

some fools think that just because we work at MTV it gives us the OK to use profanity in business conversations. Like its cool or its par for the course. In my book it shows you have no class and no consideration for others. The english language is huge. use it!

BY LESLEY FREEDMAN

Hi. I'd like to introduce myself. I'm In-House Temp **#141**. Before being chosen for this glamorous position, I spent the last four years at the university of Maryland as an english major. My expectations after graduating were high. I expected to write commercials, get published in Time magazine, and have my own assistant in one year. Now I am lucky if I get to decide to photocopy things one at a time or have them collated. Enter reality. This is my version of what it's like to be even one more step down from the low man on the totem pole.

I was very nervous to start working at MTV Networks because I thought I would type too slow,

CHUTES AND LADDERS

need a personal assistant to work the computer, or photocopy things out of order, upside down, or inside out. After being here a week I realized I had a lot more to worry about, and none of it was related to the actual work I'd be doing. Let us begin with the elevators, shall we? I'd say I spent about three hours on them the first day. At home all I've got are **STAIRS**, and at Maryland the dorm's elevator lights have been out since about 1955. I suppose this is no excuse for taking joy rides all day at MTVN. I wrongly assumed that the left light meant down and the right was up, which stems from a society teaching us that "right" and "up" are both positive words. It sounds good, huh? After being one step away from starting a concession stand on the elevator, the light bulb over my head finally turned on. Red is Hell and white is Heaven! Geez, even the elevator system here is creative. Then there's the issue of addressing people. Ms. seems too formal for a fellow co-worker and Nancy is too presumptuous, like she was my new best friend. For now I am just getting their attention with "uuummm." Also, what about inter-office mail? Ouh, who's gonna send me anything? Hallway politics are another thing.

Do I say hello to every stranger I pass? What if I say hi to the President or a ceo or something? Are we lowly interns forbidden to speak to those superiors we worship? Hey, does anyone know where I can obtain a handbook on office etiquette? I must sound like a scared little girl. Actually, I'm more than ready to jump into the lion's den, if only I knew what floor it was on. For now, although I am anxious to prove myself in more creative ways, I am trying to learn and be patient.

Although I don't have a home base just yet, I look forward to the door that will finally shut behind me rather than in front of me. For today, and maybe even tommorow and the day after that, I am simply grateful to be working for what I consider to be THE cutting edge company in New York city. And as Beavis and Butt-Head would say, "that's cool."

MTV NETWORKS
A VIACOM COMPANY

2ND annual

october 17th - 21st.

Diversity week is happening

we've talked the
talk- now let's
walk the walk!
join us each
day in the
lodge for COMEDY, DRAMA, ART, STORYTELLING AND MUSIC (snacks & prizes, too!)

MIX MATTERS #8

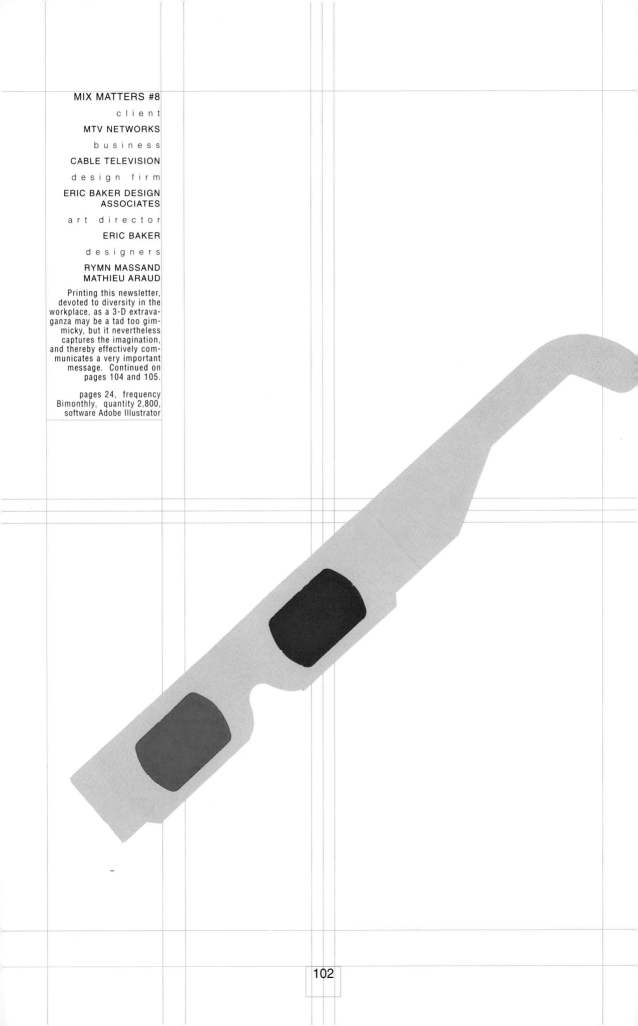

client

MTV NETWORKS

business

CABLE TELEVISION

design firm

**ERIC BAKER DESIGN
ASSOCIATES**

art director

ERIC BAKER

designers

**RYMN MASSAND
MATHIEU ARAUD**

Printing this newsletter, devoted to diversity in the workplace, as a 3-D extravaganza may be a tad too gimmicky, but it nevertheless captures the imagination, and thereby effectively communicates a very important message. Continued on pages 104 and 105.

pages 24, frequency Bimonthly, quantity 2,800, software Adobe Illustrator

mix matters

matters

mtv networks   **diversity newsletter**

#8

wednesday

On the third day Tom Freston called for less time using the word "diversity" and more time putting it in the works. He urged us to "bring in people with different points of view from different walks or places in life". Sheryl Crow strummed and sang away to a packed house.

On

tuesday

James Shaw unveiled the MTV NETWORKS Diversity poster and discussed how placing value in individual strength and characteristics makes good business sense for a company involved in foreign markets and global cultures. Vivian Warfield, Director of the New York City Art Commission discussed the role of public art in understanding distinctions within culture and introduced the "Family Album", a photography exhibit previously on view at the United Nations. And, in-house talent displayed their works -painting, poetry, illustrations, photographs - in the first ever staff art exhibit.

monday

"MTVN's 2nd Annual Celebration of Diversity began on October 17 with Gerry Laybourne pointing out the on-air manifestations of Diversity on Nickelodeon. VJ Idalis introduced tale teller and percussionist Tejumola logboni who gave listeners fresh erspectives on familiar themes such as Rock-a-bye Baby" His repertoire included w interpretations of reality.

OFFICE JOURNAL #2

client

HAWORTH, INC.

business

FURNITURE

design firm

ESSEX TWO

art director/designer

JOSEPH ESSEX

illustrator

JOSEPH ESSEX

This traditional two-color tabloid printed on semi-glossy stock is, in the argot of design, very institutional. Yet the witty collage illustration takes the edge off.

pages 8, frequency Quarterly, quantity 11,000, software QuarkXPress

Asset Management:
Benefitting Facility Management and the Bottom Line

Tapping into Strategic Alliances

Choosing the Right Information Technology

Revitalizing Offices for the '90s

office journal

2

Haworth Office Journal is a service publication from Haworth, Inc.

"'Rightsizing' your company involves the cautious match of resources to revenues ... The issue is to become smaller and stronger."

Dr. Harvey H. Kaiser is senior vice president of facilities administration at Syracuse University. He has been a facilities management consultant to higher education associations, statewide public systems and individual campuses in the U.S., Canada and Israel. Dr. Kaiser is the author of *Managing Facilities More Effectively*, *Facilities Audit Workbook* and *The Facilities Managers Reference*. He holds an undergraduate degree in architecture from Rensselaer Polytechnic Institute, and a masters degree in urban planning and a Ph.D. in social science from Syracuse University. He is registered to practice architecture in New York.

Downsizing or rightsizing? How can facilities managers find the appropriate goals and strategies when an organization must respond to cost constraints by becoming smaller?

The urgency for finding the right size for facilities management activities today is of a different nature than in the past. While the tough economic times of 15 years ago required some restructuring of organizations, the influence of a staggering national debt and a global economy is causing management to downsize operations for permanent reductions in expenditures.

The problem of finding the right size — "rightsizing" — is the cautious match of resources to revenues, of capacities to expenditures. The issue is to become smaller and stronger.

Unlike the recent past, when the facilities manager's main concerns were providing for growth and improving quality of services, there will be a need to contend with the dichotomy of simultaneous growth and reduction of activities. Some activities may be consolidated or eliminated entirely.

The facilities manager's agenda is responsiveness to dynamic change without adding space; protection of capital assets; managing space utilization effectively; and resourcefulness in managing facilities support services. The challenges for downsizing will vary as widely as the different natures of organizations and their central missions. Developing prescriptive guidelines for universal application must recognize that short-term actions may be necessary to prevent a business failure but that they must be kept in a perspective of long-term actions and policies. Artful management avoids the mindless approach of across-the-board cuts in personnel, suspending partially completed projects, and deferring facility renewal.

Downsizing should be done in increments to maintain services, plant operations and maintenance, and avoid long-term damage to facilities to be retained by the organization. Four central themes emerge from this agenda for areas of facilities management responsibilities that can be translated into organizational goals and operating strategies.

1. Responsiveness to Restructuring the Organization

Responsiveness to the restructuring of an organization is defined by the changes in how an organization does business and what reconfigurations occur in the way that it does its business. This invites a delayed response until senior management completes its restructuring and transmits its goals to operational managers. Downsizing requires special abilities to view the organization from a distant perspective and as a dynamic, evolving entity.

The fully matured role of the facilities manager is to act as a policy advisor and operations manager, moving between the boardroom and operating departments. continued on page 4

Energize!

Revitalizing Offices for the Nineties

Is your office environment obsolete? The escalation of office technology and associated communications network and cabling requirements far exceeds the standards that buildings had met just five years ago. New federal and state legislation will require facilities to have updated environmental and safety systems.

As organizations strive to be more competitive, they are seeking environments that facilitate the unique ways in which they work, in addition to environments that will help attract and retain clients and employees.

In the '90s, the overbuilt real estate market will be both a blessing and a curse. The fact of the matter is that obsolete buildings will be vacant and new, upgraded environments will attract tenants. What can facility managers, building owners, architects and engineers do to transform facilities for the well-being of its occupants? The following is a checklist to help revitalize today's office environments.

Technology Support

As personal computers, printers and other electronic devices are required in each work space, several problems can occur: there is not enough available power, or power that is available has noise or spikes; lighting can cause glare; or air conditioning systems may not be able to handle additional heat load in the space.

When planning a renovation or new building, it is important to carefully define requirements for these services for today and the next decade. Furniture manufacturers have developed products capable of carrying the sophisticated cabling and power requirements of today's offices.

Increased use of local area networks, E-mail and main frame interface require communications wiring to be properly planned to meet today's needs. Dedicated vertical distribution chases, dedicated communications closets on each floor, and adequate cable trays and raceways or raised floors for wiring should be provided.

Lighting

Besides making building interiors appear dingy, outdated interior lighting can cause assorted vision-related problems and can affect the overall efficiency of buildings. Removing older fluorescent fixtures with acrylic lenses elevates efficiency considerably. The newer fixtures also create ambient or non-glare light, enhancing light quality while reducing eye fatigue. Flexible task lighting can aid in reducing eye fatigue.

Indoor Air Quality

This past year, a bill was passed by the Senate but died in the House of Representatives to authorize a national program to reduce exposure to indoor air contaminants. New versions of the bill are being prepared for review, which are expected to be even stronger. It is also being proposed that the Environmental Protection Agency be given authority to determine adequate indoor air quality. If passed, the EPA could determine the adequacy of existing indoor air standards, assess the cost of compliance, determine the degree such standards are being adopted and encoded, and identify the extent to which buildings are being operated in a proper manner.

Ventilation

A recent update of ASHRAE Standard 62 - Ventilation for Acceptable Indoor Air Quality - has increased minimum outside air rates from 5 cfm to 15 cfm per person. Lack of adequate outside air results in recirculation of indoor air contaminants such as cigarette smoke, formaldehyde, radon, asbestos and ozone. Increasing outside air may require larger louvers and/or replacing existing outside air ductwork to air handling units, or may be accomplished by adjusting minimum damper positions on air handling units. Dedicated indoor or outdoor smoking areas will help too.

Air Circulation

Improper placement of supply air outlets and return air inlets causes air not to circulate through occupied areas. If air fails to ventilate areas where people are working, air contaminants can build up. Relocating return air grilles for non-dusted return systems is easily accomplished, while relocating supply air outlets also requires relocating ductwork. Review placement of office furniture and facility layout to maximize air circulation.

Asbestos

It is safe to assume that the majority of older buildings contain asbestos in many forms: surfacing materials, thermal system insulation and floor and ceiling tiles. Experts estimate as many as 800,000 buildings in the U.S. contain asbestos. The most dangerous form of asbestos is friable, or materials that can be crumbled, pulverized or reduced to powder by hand pressure when dry. This type of asbestos, when airborne, has been linked to various respiratory ailments. Today, laws requiring asbestos removal are limited to schools. However, when embarking upon major renovations, it is advisable to remove all asbestos.

CFCs

Fully halogenated chlorofluorocarbon (CFC) and hydrogen-containing chlorofluorocarbon (HCFC) compounds are used for a variety of applications, including refrigerants (or working fluids) in air-conditioning and refrigeration equipment, and blowing agents for thermal insulation. The Montreal Protocol, sponsored by the United Nations in September 1987, amended in June 1990 and signed by the U.S., reduces production levels of CFCs each year to reach complete phase out by the year 2000.

Last year, nearly 70 CFC-related bills were considered in 24 states, focusing on mandating the recovery and recycling of used refrigerants and prohibiting certain foam products and packaging, and the installation of insulation manufactured with CFCs.

Due to its indoor environmental impact, look for office products that contain the least amount of CFCs.

Unsafe Materials

The existence of flammable, toxic and/or combustible materials pose possible fire hazards. It is important to demolish and remove all of these materials and replace them with modern fire-safe materials. Examples of some of these are synthetic carpeting, wall coverings and certain ceiling tiles.

Furniture

Furniture design and technology has advanced greatly and many types of upgrades can be easily made. In addition to replacing old or outdated furniture, consider furniture refurbishment or trading in older pieces.

Mechanical Systems

Outdated mechanical systems undermine building efficiency because of the inability to handle current and future loads. Poorly designed systems can become breeding grounds for viruses, microbes and other organisms. Humidifier pans, cooling coil drain pans and low points in duct systems are sources of stagnant water that must be properly drained. Properly designed or modified systems can lower the potential of these hazards and lower maintenance costs.

Building Cooling Towers

Cooling towers, evaporative condensers, humidifiers, potable water heaters and holding tanks, pipes containing stagnant warm water, shower heads, faucet aerators and whirlpool baths provide conditions suitable for the growth and multiplication of legionella or Legionnaire's Disease. Design and good housekeeping procedures that prevent amplification and dissemination of Legionnaire's Disease should be formulated and implemented before systems are operated.

Energy Conservation

Many buildings were constructed considering only first costs. Buildings need energy cost reduction measures that could include airside economizer cycles, waterside economizer cycles, variable frequency drivers on pumps, primary-secondary pumping and chilled water or ice storage.

Building Automation Systems

Building automation systems have improved dramatically over the past 10 years. Systems should be capable of proportional-integral-derivative or PID controls to permit distributed control to mechanical equipment rooms. PID controls allow anticipatory action to the controller that result in faster responses and greater stability.

Security Systems

Six top security concerns are 1) employee theft, 2) substance abuse, 3) property crime, 4) liability insurance, 5) violent crime and 6) white collar crime. To fight these concerns buildings should have electronic access controls, closed circuit television, security lighting and security guards.

Fire Protection Systems

Many older buildings were constructed without sprinkler systems. Buildings should have comprehensive fire protection systems including smoke detectors, heat detectors, sprinkler systems and fire alarm systems. Public address systems should be located throughout buildings for use during an emergency. Stair pressurization systems should be present on all buildings over three floors. A "zone of refuge" area as part of the fire stairs provides refuge for handicapped employees.

Core Configurations

An inadequate configuration of common core elements results in inefficient use of the building's footprint as well as creating additional non-usable circulation space. By reconfiguring the shared tenant floor elements, an order may be established to allow more tenant lease space as well as simplified circulation flow. If done properly, adequate space may be gained to allow for common vending or copy areas for tenants.

Movement

Outdated vertical circulation can cause long waits during morning, noon and evening hours. An evaluation of elevator loading and usage requirements is helpful to determine vertical transportation deficiencies for a building. These deficiencies can be at least partially overcome by adding escalators at high traffic lower levels and modernizing elevator equipment and electronics. Reviewing office adjacencies, aisleways and other facility traffic elements can reduce office cycle time.

Americans with Disabilities Act (ADA)

The ADA, effective January, 1992, protects workers with disabilities by stipulating requirements that will allow them to properly complete their day-to-day activities with the same ease as workers with no disabilities. Handicap issues are no longer controlled by code officials — they are controlled by a court of law. Code variances are not allowed. This impacts access to buildings, office designs restrooms, emergency signs and doorways, among other things.

For example, physical barriers in existing facilities must be removed or alternative methods of providing services must be offered. And, all new construction in public and commercial facilities must be accessible.

Shared Facilities

In older buildings, restrooms, drinking fountains and stairs typically have not been well maintained and need thorough upgrading. Toilets, partitions, lavatory tops and drinking fountains should be replaced with newer, more durable ones. When replacing these items, it might be a good time to retrofit for expanded handicap accessibility. Stairs should be carefully examined for compliance with current codes.

Appearance

When finishes in tenant-common areas of older buildings have yellowed, often a new coat of paint is not enough. As tenants become more sophisticated, so do their clientele. As new buildings provide newer, brighter tenant areas, older buildings should follow suit. Both tenants and clients expect it.

Many buildings constructed from the mid-1950s through the 1970s are badly in need of thorough remodeling to convey a desirable image in public spaces and building exteriors. Building owners can replace the "skin" of buildings, upgrade landscapes, signage and parking features, and renovate lobbies, elevator cabs and other high traffic areas. Internal assets such as furniture, fabrics and finish colors can also be upgraded.

Tenant Amenities

Older buildings typically lack the modern convenience of newer buildings such as shared tenant services, retail facilities, food service, banking, daycare and health clubs. Depending on locations, building sites away from commercial business districts need to provide more of these amenities. As employers become more aware of the value of preventive health care and the need to relieve stress, they will seek accessibility to fitness and convenience facilities as part of the workplace.

"Revitalizing Offices for the 90s" is a collaborative effort by members of CRSS Architecture, Houston. Authors include Steven A. Parshall, AIA, Senior Vice President; Conny R. Brown, P.E., Vice President, Director of Engineering Programming; and Mark Herman, Interior Designer.

new ways
From Hexcel Corporation

Imaginative Solutions. Nearly 50 years ago, from a basement laboratory in Northern California, Hexcel introduced structural Honeycomb, the first of its innovative high-technology products. Honeycomb soon revolutionized the aerospace industry by making aircraft lighter, safer and stronger. Today Hexcel continues to integrate technology, innovation and imagination by offering new solutions for improving overall product performance.

Honeycomb and Advanced Composite materials have likewise revolutionized the recreation equipment market. From athletic shoes to sailboats, Hexcel's materials make sports equipment lighter and stronger, providing enthusiasts with a competitive edge.

With a focus on safety and economy, Hexcel's new generation of recyclable, thermoplastic honeycomb provides lightweight components that offer new design freedom and improved passenger saftey in the transportation industries.

The ability to offer creative solutions to design and manufacturing problems has been crucial to Hexcel's success. And this magazine is a celebration of the successful collaborations among Hexcel and its customers during the last half-century. On these pages you'll see that imaginative solutions are behind every story of innovation and achievement.

Out of this world

Revolutionizing telecommunications
Satellites that form the basis of a revolutionary new global telecommunications system rely on lightweight, high strength carbon fiber prepregs from Hexcel.

The Iridium System™, a $3.45 billion telecommunications system being built by Motorola's Satellite Communications Division, will use 66 cross-linked low Earth orbit satellites to form a wireless personal communications network providing users with instantaneous, global telephone transmissions—including voice, data, fax and paging.

Lockheed Missiles & Space Co., Sunnyvale, CA., under contract to provide the spacecraft bus, systems engineering support, satellite vehicle assembly, integration and test support for the project, selected Hexcel's high modulus carbon fiber interdirectional tape and unidirectional fiber for the bus structure, because of its maximum design strength and minimum weight. Each spacecraft is expected to weigh about 1500 pounds.

Tom Tadano, Lockheed's Iridium director, said, "Hexcel was a natural choice to supply composite materials for the project, because we have a long history together, and a large database on this particular resin

system. Hexcel's R&D facility has been extraordinarily fast at developing small fabric samples for testing, too. It all adds up to reliability—essential to a project of such magnitude."

The contract to provide materials used in the Iridium System satellite bus structure will play an important role in gaining recognition and widespread acceptance for new applications of Hexcel's state-of-the-art carbon fiber prepregs.

page **2**
Recreation
Faster, stronger, tougher

page **4**
Aerospace
Making aerospace history

page **6**
Transportation
Designing performance

NEW WAYS
client
HEXCEL
business
FURNITURE
design firm
COLEMAN SOUTER DESIGN
art director
MARK COLEMAN
designers
ERIK WATTS
DAVID NONG

This four-color newsletter employs a variety of magazine conceits, including well-designed referral lines, silhouetted photographs, and various surprints and overprints—all well paced and consistent.

pages 8, software QuarkXPress

Faster, lighter, tougher

"There are many advantages in using Hexcel Composites in Cobra's golf shafts. One of these is strength—shafts of Hexcel material always extend our strength requirements. Hexcel's service and support team are unsurpassed, too: they're always there for me."

Rich Reyes, Plant Manager, Cobra Golf Inc.

Taking a Swing at the Golf Market...
In the not-too-distant future, carbon and glass-and-carbon hybrids will replace steel shafts in the majority of drivers and irons. Their increased impact toughness and load dampening characteristics are improvements over traditional steel shafts. Equally important, individually tailored carbon shafts can improve the performance of beginning and expert golfers alike.

A preferred supplier to top-of-the line Taylor Made®, Cobra® Golf, and other premium golf club manufacturers, Hexcel supplies unidirectional tape—used in shaft manufacturing—that meets extraordinarily tight, consistent quality standards. Our ability to integrate materials and technologies to achieve improved impact toughness, appearance and durability, and our manufacturing efficiencies and lower scrap rates make our products not only cost-competitive, but often less expensive than competing suppliers.

Skis were the jumping off point for Hexcel's involvement in the recreational market, back in the 70s. Since then, advanced materials have revolutionized the recreational equipment market. From skis and snowboards to golf clubs and athletic shoes, Hexcel's remarkable materials and technologies have made equipment—and the athletes who use it—faster, lighter and tougher.

Here are just a few of the many applications of Hexcel materials:

Mad About Hexcel
"A canoe is a unique engineering challenge," says Kathryn W. Ivery, president of Mad River Canoe. "It must withstand impacts, abrasion and considerable stress; be light enough to carry, yet strong enough to hold over 20 times its own weight in passengers and gear. All the while, it must be fun to paddle, and beautiful to behold. Over the years, Hexcel has worked with us to develop the special fabrics that give our canoes all these qualities and more—and we continue to work together in our quest for the ultimate canoe."

Making a Splash
If flexibility is the key, Australia are a thing of beauty—in and out of the water. And, they're more likely to stay that way because the skis and boards are made with Hexcel's specially engineered Nomex®, which are less likely to chip or scratch their paint. Cool, too, because Hexcel's materials dissipate heat from the board's high-performance core, reducing heat damage.

King of the Mountain. . .
Though Hexcel no longer has a brand name ski, we're still at the forefront of ski technology through our partnership with renowned European ski manufacturer Salomon.

Hexcel's fiberglass prepreg, used as the structural skin wrapping the core of Salomon skis, has helped achieve higher performance at lower weights than commonly used wet layup processes—while keeping prices affordable. That's because our rapid cure resin requires just 15 minutes at 180 degrees, compared with many prepregs that require up to 100 degrees and several hours to cure.

Fast On Our Feet...
Reebok was the first—and is still one of the few—athletic shoe manufacturers using the technical advantages of honeycomb and advanced composites to achieve higher performance. Our Hexalite® honeycomb replaces the foam formerly used in the heel and ball of Reebok's mid-to-higher ($50+) priced shoes, thereby reducing weight, increasing energy absorption and improving resistance to fatigue and compaction. And, Hexcel-designed and manufactured arch bridges shave vital ounces from their top-of-the-line running shoes, while maintaining necessary foot support and flexibility.

Reebok, a $3 billion-plus company, initially contacted Hexcel as a possible alternate source for composites already used in its shoes. The request represented a new challenge for Hexcel: fusion welding honeycomb to the skins instead of using customary adhesive bonding systems. Despite requiring a completely new manufacturing process, Hexcel supplied samples in well under six months, and was in full production within a year.

Now, Hexcel and Reebok have a thriving partnership. When Reebok's product engineers first suggested a weight-saving composite arch bridge, Hexcel's Prototyping Center engineers used state-of-the-art CAD/CAM modeling techniques to turn concept into reality. Then, they designed a fabric architecture and quick cure resin system, developed a production process and shipped parts inside of six months. Now, Hexcel engineers routinely help Reebok evaluate new technologies. The "one-stop shopping" offered by our integrated manufacturing capabilities clearly has made us "faster, lighter and tougher" than the competition.

HOMART

client

HOMART

business

REAL ESTATE DEVELOPMENT

design firm

CONCRETE

designers

**JILLY SIMONS
DAVID ROBSON**

photographer

THOMAS HEINSER

This four-color glossy magazine is the high-end of the
spectrum. No detail is over-
looked in this well-designed
format.

pages 24, frequency
Biannually, quantity 6,500,
software QuarkXPress

NEWS!

client

OLYMPIA AND YORK COMPANIES

business

REAL ESTATE MANAGEMENT & DEVELOPMENT

design firm

DRENTTEL DOYLE PARTNERS

art director

STEPHEN DOYLE

designer

ROSEMARIE TURK

This two-color, newspaper-like publication printed on a toothy, textured paper stock is notable for the large variety of typefaces used throughout. The type provides both information and a certain decorative relief.

pages 8, frequency Quarterly, quantity 30,000-35,000, software QuarkXPress

DIALOGUE

client

PHAMIS INC.

business

HEALTH CARE

design firm

THE TRAVER COMPANY

art director

ALLEN WOODARD

designer

NANCY KINNEAR

On the quarterfold of this black-and-white tabloid is a bold image and logo that shouts at the reader. When unfolded the image is repeated with even more prominence. While a seemingly excessive use of visuals for a four-page newsletter, its graphic strength grabs attention.

pages 4, frequency Quarterly, quantity 1,000, software Aldus PageMaker

A newsletter for type enthusiasts
from Typographic Resource

Contents
A brief history of Berthold, 1858-1983.
How Berthold adapts Monotype Plantin
from metal into phototype.
Typeface quality by Günter Gerhard
Lange, art director of Berthold.
Classification of typefaces by period.
Text and headline faces available from
Typographic Resource.
The new Tr. type gauge.

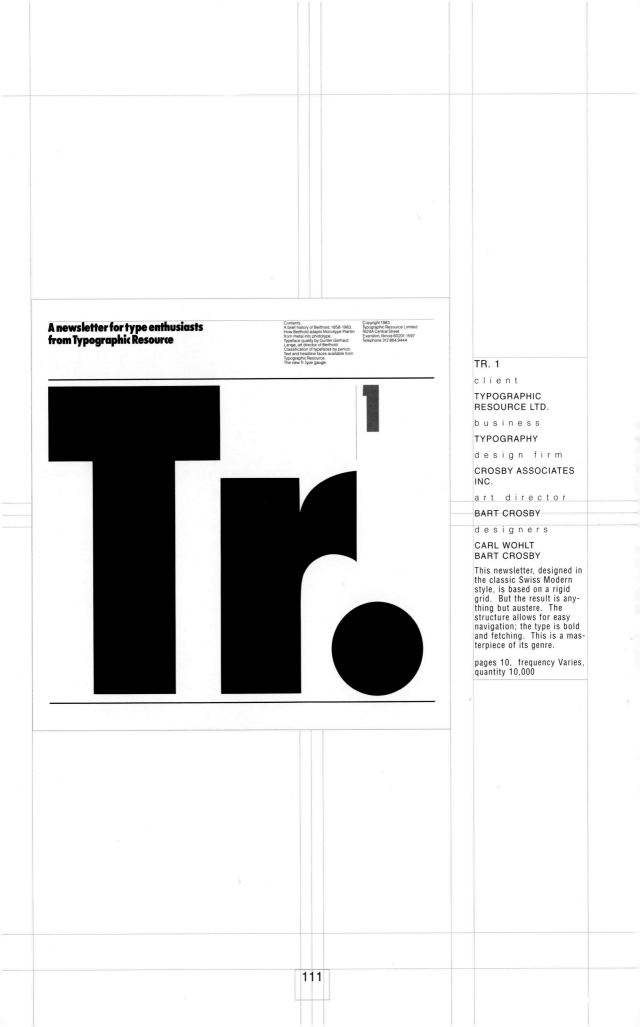

Tr. 1

TR. 1

client
**TYPOGRAPHIC
RESOURCE LTD.**

business
TYPOGRAPHY

design firm
**CROSBY ASSOCIATES
INC.**

art director
BART CROSBY

designers
**CARL WOHLT
BART CROSBY**

This newsletter, designed in
the classic Swiss Modern
style, is based on a rigid
grid. But the result is anything but austere. The
structure allows for easy
navigation; the type is bold
and fetching. This is a masterpiece of its genre.

pages 10, frequency Varies,
quantity 10,000

PENTASPEAK

client

PENTAGRAM DESIGN

business

DESIGN CONSULTANCY

design firm

PENTAGRAM DESIGN

designers

**PAULA SCHER
DAVID HILLMAN**

Newsletters are often used to sell a design firm's key attributes to clients and other designers. This magazine format not only showcases the firm's annual output, but frames it in a journal that further exemplifies the firm's talents.

pages 20, frequency Annually, quantity 5,000, software QuarkXPress

The Work
of the Pentagram
Partners in
London, New York,
and San Francisco

Pentaspeak

The **3** rd Dimension

The second edition of Pentaspeak is devoted to the third dimension. While the majority of Pentagram's designers work in graphics, many also create products, buildings and environmental designs. In this issue we present projects that express both our graphic sensibilities and our understanding of form.

For the Tate Gallery in London, Pentagram proposed this flexible and mobile sign system to carry directions and information and to act as a poster site for temporary exhibitions. The signs were made of epoxy-resin coated steel with decal lettering.
David Hillman
Jo Swindell

Pentagram was established over twenty years ago on a foundation of multi-disciplinary design talents. We came together as partners because we believed we would continue to educate and stimulate one another and thereby provide superior services to our clients and the larger community.

Because we are a collection of designers trained in a variety of disciplines, Pentagram frequently has the opportunity to provide a client with more than one type of expertise. Collaboration among the different disciplines is the very core of the partnership; when the partners collaborate, every level of the design is driven by a single central idea, theme and visual message.

While our design backgrounds and specialities are diverse, we share similar convictions about our work. We are dedicated to quality and intelligence in design; not through one rigid ideology but through a clear understanding of the problem at hand and a desire to solve it with a fresh and often previously untried solution. We approach our work with a combination of analysis and passion.

When we develop a product, we fulfill functional requirements first and then aim to supply intangible rewards like sensuousness or amusement. When we plan a building or revitalize an interior, we strive to create a special place: a house may become a tribute to its occupants, a store may become a stage for merchandise. When we develop a sign system, we make clarity our first goal and then add visual wit or sculptural form. We begin with a package as a protective container and then develop it one step further; it may also become a movable display or a beautifully wrapped gift.

The projects represented in this issue are commercial and experimental, intimate and industrial. They represent professional jobs we've done for profit and personal things we've made for fun. All of these activities are based on the philosophy that when we satisfy ourselves, chances are, we will satisfy others too.

The Hair Brush was part of a series Wendy Pirbe created for an exhibition called "Alphabet City" at the Illustration Gallery in New York. Wendy Pirbe

In this issue we are happy to introduce two new partners in our London office: David Pocknell, graphic and interior designer, and Daniel Weil, architect and industrial designer.

David Pocknell joins Pentagram from the successful design practice he started in Britain in 1964. Well known and respected throughout the design industry, he is the immediate past President of the Chartered Society of Designers and a Fellow of the Society of Typographic Designers. He is design consultant to London Transport and the TSB Bank, among others, and has received a gold award from the New York Art Directors Club and a Minerva Award from the Chartered Society of Designers.

Daniel Weil will be combining his new position at Pentagram with his post as Professor of Industrial & Vehicle Design at the Royal College of Art in London. Daniel, who trained as an architect in his native Argentina, came to Britain in 1978 to study industrial design at the Royal College, then ran a partnership with Gerald Taylor from 1985 to 1990. His idiosyncratic and experimental work has caught the imagination of manufacturers like Alessi and Knoll and his work is in the permanent collections of the Museum of Modern Art, New York and the Victoria & Albert Museum, London. His architectural and interior projects range from television stage sets to retail interiors and private residences.

Originally a personal logotype for Mr. and Mrs. Aubrey Hair of Dallas, this comb was made into a three-dimensional shop sign for the "Alphabet City" exhibition. Wendy Pirbe

The products on this page were designed and developed by Kenneth Grange and his design team at Pentagram's London office.

The Kompakt Design Razor created by Pentagram for Wilkinson Sword. Spare blades are carried in the handle, giving rise to a distinctive appearance. The handle of the all-metal product is sleeved in textured rubber to give a good grip.

British Rail InterCity 125 locomotive (scale model)

Polaroid "Image" Sunglasses

Kenwood KT 450 steam iron

Proposal for the Channel Tunnel Passenger Train

Wilkinson Sword's Royale twin swivel blade razor incorporates a refined mechanism for picking up and disposing of blades. A plated die-cast zinc handle with inserted rubber grip gives the razor a tactile quality and the reassuring weight of a well-crafted tool.

Kenwood JE100 Juice Extractor

The design of Platignum's Platpen series takes its principal character from the clip, initially inspired by the traditional stainless steel drawing board clip used by draughtsmen for the past forty years. The result is a design that is visually distinctive in the marketplace.

Cast as one piece in aluminum, the Thorpac ice cream scoop is available in a choice of natural finish or black Teflon coating. The design of the scoop invests this mundane product with a certain elegance and balance.

Thorpac

Shiseido "Tansly" men's toiletries

The Wilkinson Sword Protector razor includes a new safety feature in blade construction: fine wires have been woven closely across the cutting edges of the two blades to protect the skin from nicks and cuts. The Protector's handle is weighted and padded to add a sense of security in handling, and its bright red color is deliberately bold to support the robust, sculptural form. The product name draws attention to its unique level of safety.

"Lagata" uplighter for Thorn Lighting

Kenwood FP700 food processor

This brushed stainless steel pen is one of the Parker 25 range designed for the lower price sector of the pen market. The range includes a steel-nibbed fountain pen with cartridge ink refills, a retracting ballpoint pen and a fibre-tipped pen.

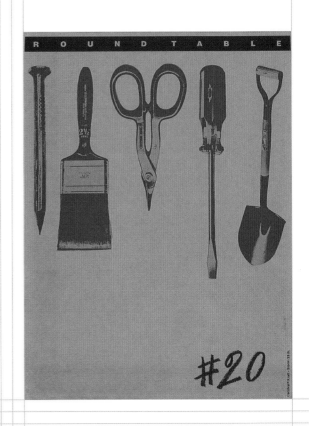

ROUNDTABLE
client
CHAMPION
INTERNATIONAL
business
PAPER COMPANY
design firm
MIHO
designer
MIHO
photographers
SALLY BRUCE
MICHAEL STEINBERG

The delightful use of object
or still-life photography
helps give this newsletter
with coordinated envelope
the aura of an annual report.
Continued on pages 116
through 119.

pages 20, quantity 10,000,
software QuarkXPress

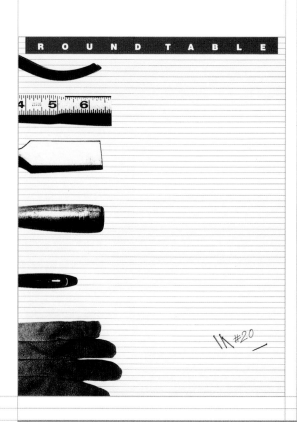

Prombo explains that bulletins and checklists, which make up 60 percent of the work, follow a regular schedule and a consistent format, and run on the same presses each week. When it comes to other work, however, customers now fill out requisitions. These requisitions serve as job tickets when boards are sent to Downers Grove. "Administrative services automatically writes in a five-day turnaround," Prombo says, "and although we can usually beat that, the five days gives us a buffer. The important thing is that our customers can know what to expect. And if, for some reason, we can't make a due date, there's a basis on which to negotiate."

A full-time scheduler now schedules all work and tracks every job as it goes through the shop. "But we also send her to Oak Brook," says Prombo, "once or twice a week. First, she visits administrative services to iron out problems in the regular schedule and scout out jobs that may require special papers or inks. Then she drops in on regular customers just to see what's up, and advises people who use us less often on the procedures involved.

"The benefit of this practice," he adds, "is a vast improvement in communications. Customers tell us rapport with reprographics is better than ever before."

One tool that has been of immense help is the reprographic customer's instruction guide which describes the printing processes available and provides samples of headline type and paper grades. The paper shades are often used to color-key Ace categories: "When a dealer gets a bulletin, he can tell right away if pages concern lumber or lawn and garden." In other cases, where paper selection is less well prescribed, "the guide enables our customers to get an idea of what they'd like.

Carnival Kraft, Stone/28 lb.

"Once they make an initial selection, we sit down and advise them," he continues. "If they choose an expensive sheet, we explain how much it will cost, and we might try to show how we can create the same mood with the proper inks and a lesser grade.

"Overall, though, the aim of the book is customer awareness and education. It enhances our productivity because the customer becomes part of that picture. If he changes his mind, or orders things we don't have, it can slow us down considerably."

In building its staff, meanwhile, the reprographics division has followed a practice of promoting, whenever possible, from within. Indeed, notes Prombo, "nearly all of today's employees have moved up through the ranks of this shop." The result, he says, "is a work force that is both loyal and imaginative. Most of our changes have come from direct employee input." he points out. "What's more, in the course of moving from clerical positions to camera, bindery,

and press, our people become completely familiar with the requirements of our work. Our operators know the difference," Prombo says. "They're so clear about our priorities that we leave the responsibility for quality control pretty much up to them."

Reprographics also instituted a procedure to track productivity and provide regular feedback to their employees. Within six months, pressroom productivity was up by 25 percent. "We think our people were challenged when they had something to compare themselves to," he says. "It motivated them, just being aware of how they stacked up against the average."

In addition, departmental and interdepartmental meetings are held once a month to discuss problems, productivity, and quality control. And every three months, meetings bring together employees from the

first and second shifts. Nevertheless, Prombo contends that the most valuable conversations take place daily, during the 15 minutes the two shifts overlap. "Although one could view it as wasted production time," he says, "it gives these people a chance to talk. It fosters cooperation between the shifts, and we think that really pays off."

The future of the division, says Prombo, will include a large measure of cooperation with the company's data processing department. "In-plant managers tend to get territorial these days," he observes, "but there's no point to conflict and competition. When Ace looked into purchasing a Xerox 9700* (now in the Oak Brook computer room), we were part of the planning committee. We taught data processing a lot about printing,

and discussed both their limitations and our own. The end result was that we agreed to enhance each other in a way that worked to the benefit of the dealers."

With regard to reprographics, the 9700's primary mission will be producing camera-ready art, replacing work now done by word processors and mechanical artists. With a Xerox 1050* graphics option, all graphics used in Ace checklists are now being scanned and digitized. "Once that's done," says Prombo, "we'll call up graphics and text and merge them automatically."

*Xerox 9700, and 1050 are trademarks of Xerox Corporation.

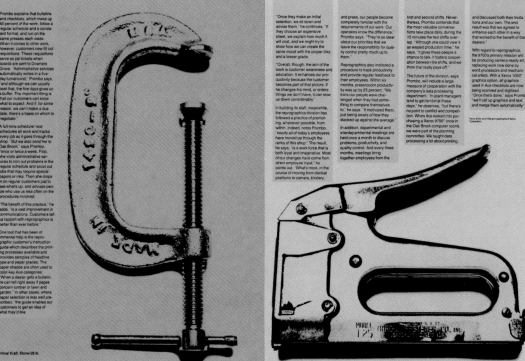

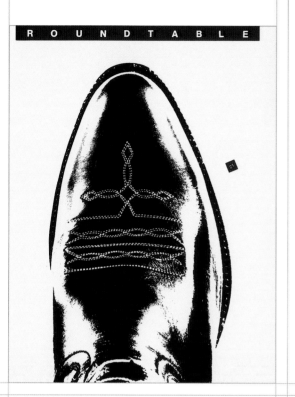

ROUNDTABLE NOTES

Once considered the workhorse of the in-plant print shop, offset lithography is caught in the crosscurrents of an industry-wide revolution. With the advent of sophisticated high-speed copiers and electronic printers, much of what was traditionally reserved for offset is now more effectively produced by other means.

In light of technology's rapid encroachment of offset territory, in-plant printers are taking a hard look at their offset applications with an eye toward their increasingly specialized requirements and the inevitable bottom line. Does offset have a place in the in-plant print shop of the future? And, if so, what will it be?

Ron Baxley, manager of in-house print facilities for Republic Financial Services, Inc., of Dallas, Texas, faced these issues early on. In an article for ROUNDTABLE, Baxley suggests that the key to successful in-plant printing is not a question of either/or but of co-existence—assigning the right process to the right task.

Rather than threatening traditional values in printing, advancing technology is allowing offset to do what it does best: to produce a winning combination of high-quality work and a sense of pride in one's craft.

As odd as it sounds, it more than seems that way, doesn't it? It was not all that long ago that printers were searching for a way to reproduce the customer photograph. Join us as "Through the Printer's Loupe" takes a close-up look at halftone printing including some of its history and its wealth of exciting visual effects. At little expense and with a touch of imagination, you'll be surprised at what you did!

Focusing even further on the offset theme, our three panelists from Zale Corporation, Mary Kay Cosmetics, and Glen Mills address how they are tailoring their in-plant shops, personnel, and other capabilities to better meet their parent company's growing needs. Join them for this lively and informative discussion on how they are serving on top of the communications revolution.

This issue of ROUNDTABLE also proves several Champion promotional pieces which are yours for the asking. Simply check with your local Champion merchant representative. From The Printing Salesman's Herald, Book 45 to our Pinelands® Offset promotion, Champion's commitment to quality helps uphold your commitment to high professional standards. ★

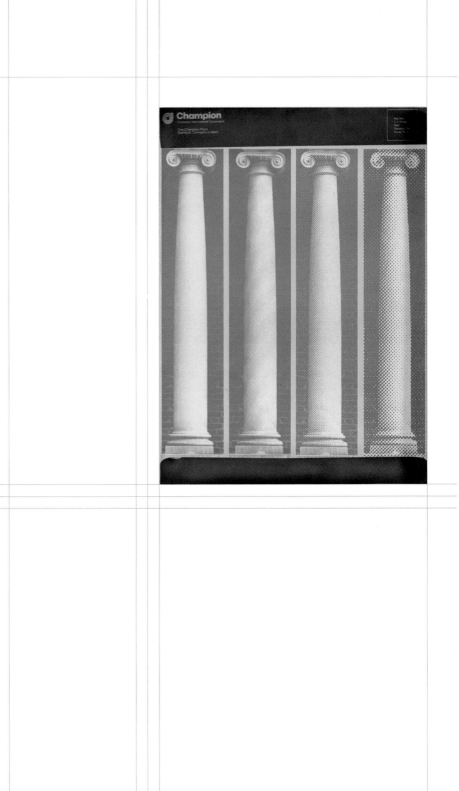

22

NOTES

forms
forms
forms
forms
forms
forms

When Benjamin Franklin noted that nothing is certain but death and taxes, he might well have added forms to that list. Indeed there's no escaping them. We are, after all, a society of information seekers. We have come to depend upon our "write here," "check there" way of life as the most efficient means of transferring details about ourselves and what we do from one source to another.

With the advent of the computer, techno-prophets predicted an end to forms and the dawning of a new, paperless society. That age has yet to begin. Despite the increased speed with which we can now process information and the host of spin-off advances in equipment, technology, ink, and paper, the form remains, even flourishes, as the standard tool of business operations.

Consider for a moment the recent estimate that every man, woman, and child in America on average has to deal with no less than two pounds of forms a year. Now multiply that by 230 million if you want to see some impressive figures!

This issue of Roundtable takes a look at the business of forms from a number of in-plant perspectives. Need to create a form but you're not quite sure where to start? Leslie Matthies, executive director of the Management Research Society and an authority on forms design, offers several tips on improving the efficiency of your forms by learning to avoid those documents that have been "authored" rather than "designed."

George Bunn, manager of in-plant printing at the Christian Broadcasting Network in Virginia Beach, Virginia, discusses his operation as it applies to the growing business of computerized mass mailing. Instead of waiting on the sidelines to see what develops with this new forms technology, CBN is establishing new production records and quite a name for itself as a pioneer in this exciting new field for in-plants.

Roundtable also features three mini-interviews with Disney World, Dun & Bradstreet Plan Services, and Mid-Florida Technical Institute which focus on the similarities and differences in their forms production and what each has in store for the future of their respective shops.

"Through the Printer's Loupe" presents several forms tools and definitions which are basic to good design. Armed with the appropriate equipment and a well-thought-out plan of action, there's no reason why your next forms job cannot be a classic.

Notice our new look? This issue of Roundtable offers only a sampling of Champion's new line of Carnival® colors — a winning combination of old favorites and completely new colors that put a rainbow at your fingertips. Also introduced is the new Champion® Linen line, Champion's new Carnival Opaque Offset and Carnival Opaque Cover, and new shades for Champion Register Bond and MICR Bond. Promotional pieces and printing demonstrations on the new Carnival line are yours for the asking. Simply check with your local Champion merchant representative for more details. From one end of the spectrum to the other, Champion makes you look like a pro.

"Half the News That's Fit to Print"

The Cheap-o Times

Benefit™ Natural, Flax

PARODY EDITION

Today: Partly cloudy, low-pressure front, showers, low 61.
Tomorrow: Overcast, no sun, less of everything. High 62.
Yesterday: Gone forever.

SUNDAY

TWO CENTS

Speed of Light Reduced to 55,000 m.p.s.

By Jack Nicholson Dimes

A purloined highway sign outside the National Physics Resources Lab in Huntsville, Ala., reads: SPEED LIMIT 55 ($\times 10^3$ mps)—WE MEAN IT!

The NPR's announcement last week that new research showed the speed of light to be 55,000 miles per second, less than a third of the old 186,000 mps, has sent the scientific community into a galaxy-sized tizzy. Not only will the most basic equations of modern physics have to be recalculated, but the whole notion that the speed of light is a universal constant is being questioned, since it appears to vary in different environments. In some rural areas, according to NPR's results, the speed of light can rise to 65 ($\times 10^3$) mps.

One obvious question: could the old figure and the new one both be correct? Says TV astronomer and male model Carl Sagan, "It's possible the speed of light is simply slowing down. Everything else is. And this would explain something we astronomers have been noticing—everything seems a lot *dimmer* than it did a few years back."

Anecdotal evidence suggests Sagan may be right. Phone companies using fiber optics in their systems report an upsurge in "burping-phone syndrome": phones which ring for longer than they should in a dull flatulent tone. (A sure sign of a slowed signal.) And rock promoters report complaints that the lasers used in rock concerts seem droopy and limp.

Others, particularly ecologists, pooh-pooh Sagan's slow-down theory. They say the speed of light is what it always was, but that it's being slowed by airborne pollution. This would explain the 55–65 ($\times 10^3$) disparity between urban and rural areas. Stephen Hawking, the "father" of modern physics, goes even further. His posit: there may be no such thing as light. Light, says Hawking, may be just "an absence of darkness." He points out there is observably a lot more darkness than light in the universe. This in turn would mean that what we perceive as stars, novas, quasars, etc., are actually intensely concentrated absences of darkness, or as he dubs them, "white holes."

To be sure, theories of the universe are in for a drubbing. Some astrophysicists are reacting badly. One British stargazer had to be forcibly removed from the podium during a lecture at the Royal Academy, when he began insisting that the universe was actually an elephant standing on the back of a turtle.

More pragmatically, the new speed means that a light-year is only one third the distance it was. Thus everything in the universe is much nearer than was supposed. Budget-minded Congressmen are taking a long hard look at NASA's space program; for the first time the "space walk" looks like more than a media stunt. "We're not saying deep-space probes won't still have to travel substantial distances," says Bob Dole (R. Kans.). "On the other hand it may now be possible to walk to Mars on the weekend."

Ironically, government cuts may be behind the whole furor. NPR, like most nonmilitary research centers, has been seriously underfunded for years. (Several work-stations in the Lab sport hand-lettered signs reading: "Government-Funded Scientist. Homeless and Hungry. Please Help.") And while Dr. John Jekyll, NPR's boss, strenuously denies it, there is a persistent rumor that the crucial experiment which led to the revised speed of light involved a stopwatch, a piece of string and a flashlight.

THE NEW SPEED OF LIGHT: WHAT IT MEANS TO YOU

Shorter Week

Proposal is to drop days from the work rather than shorten all seven. (Surveys show, Monday, Wednesday least popular days.)

The New Week:

Sunday, Tuesday, Thursday, Friday, Saturday.

Dimmer Spectrum

Colors will fade across the spectrum.

The New Spectrum

1. Sorta Red
2. Orangish
3. Yellowish
4. Greenish
5. Bluish
6. Indigoish
7. Kinda Violet

Weaker Light

One lumen will represent only a third of its present power. Lighting will become prohibitive.

Sample Effects:

To light fridge—300-watt bulb. To operate high beams: two extra 9/12-volt batteries (four for BMWs with fog lights).

Altered Relativity

$E = mc^2$ will have a different value with "c" less than a third what it is now. We will still have nine times less energy and/or weigh nine times as much.

Fainter Moon

Decreased light from sun will make moon almost invisible. Effects of moon will disappear, including tides and drastic mood swings.

GOOD 5¢ CIGAR

S. SCHWAST

New Jersey to Cut Back, New York to Close Up

By Harrison Fraud

"No New is good New," quipped Governor Jim Florio of (New) Jersey at a press conference in Trenton yesterday. As part of his slash-and-burn cutbacks in state spending, Florio announced that he was dropping the word "New" from his state's name.

"The only people who still call it *New* Jersey are anti-tax bumper-sticker writers," added the governor from a bullet-proof Plexiglas box surrounded by state troopers with tactical nuclear weapons. "Anyone sane calls it Jersey, and Jersey it's gonna be."

The name change will mean immediate savings, claimed Florio. (New) Jersey—outside of California, the nation's most regulated state—has over a million regulations in force in various fields and a form for every one. Last year alone the state printed more than a trillion forms.

Dropping a mere four characters (including the space) from these means a printing savings in the hundreds of thousands. Paper costs will plummet, too—even though Jersey currently prints its forms on recycled paper towels. Hundreds of tons of recycled paper will thus be freed up for further use as kitchen towels, making Jersey, in Florio's memorable if mysterious words: "the quickest picker-upper of the fifty states."

Mayor David Dinkins of New York City announced later the same day that he, too, was phasing out the word "New" from his city's name. "Except for Japanese tourists and Bill Buckley, 'New York' hasn't been pronounced as two words for a century," said Dinkins. He proposed a two-stage conversion, first dropping the space between "New" and "York," then after six months dropping the "ew" to form the "phonetically correct" "Nyork." The city, another ferocious form-printer, will realize a similar savings in printing and paper costs.

The mayor, who in 18 months has not received a single favorable media story, was immediately condemned by Governor Cuomo. Cuomo labelled the move "me-too-ism," adding that the day New York started getting its ideas from Jersey was the "day to take a long walk off a short pier." He called the plan "stupid," "cretinous" and "cynical," but praised Dinkins for his "personal courage," "quiet dignity" and "terrific taste in tennis gear."

The mayor was unavailable to respond at press time, being too busy with plans for a five-borough bake sale to raise funds to offset the city's budget shortfall. He intends to unveil a new recipe at the sale—a gift to his "beloved hometown." It's for something called "Dinkin Donuts."

Murray, you SOB, you left me for that floozy Miriam, and you stiffed me for the rent! Pay up you CHEAPSKATE! —ADVT.

Well-known public figure points out name changes in nation's two most bankrupt states on cheap blackboard.

NEW JERSEY
NEW YORK

Middle East Cancelled

By Less Walesa

In an unprecedented inter-network agreement, CBS, NBC, ABC, Fox, PBS and CNN have decided to cancel the Middle East.

"Last spring it was Twin Peaks and David Lynch," said Bob Iger, head of programming for ABC, "and we had 'em. This spring it was the Mideast and Peter Jennings—and we had them, too."

But, Iger pointed out, Twin Peaks is currently languishing in the cellar at No. 101 in the ratings, and media planners feel the Mideast is headed the same way.

What effect the cancellation will have on the Mideast itself is unclear. State Dept. officials worry that Israel, long accustomed to being the center of attention in the contentious Mideast family, may throw a serious tantrum. Possibly even a nuclear one. Saddam Hussein, by contrast, who is fond of the old maxim that there's no such thing as bad publicity, may finally self-destruct. Says Margaret Tutwiler of State, "Cancellation may achieve what military victory couldn't."

In a related development, General Norman Schwarzkopf admitted to the House Armed Services Committee that several of the best action sequences from the Gulf War were actually taped in the Mojave, months prior to Operation Desert Storm. He also cleared up a question which has been asked by many—how come no one had heard of him before last August? The answer: Mr. Schwarzkopf is not a general at all, but an actor who does voice-overs for radio and TV spots. His bluff, raspy tones have been well known to tens of millions of Americans for years.

FRANCE

Inexpensive tourist brochure map, completely irrelevant to story, replaces more expensive and more detailed map of area known as the Middle East.

THE CHEAP-O TIMES

client

CHAMPION
INTERNATIONAL CORP.

business

PAPER COMPANY

design firm

PENTAGRAM DESIGN

designer

PAULA SCHER

illustrator

SEYMOUR CHWAST

This tabloid paper promotion
was distributed at a national
design conference. A parody of a newspaper, it was
designed to exhibit the durability of the paper company's
least expensive paper stock.

pages 6, quantity 15,000

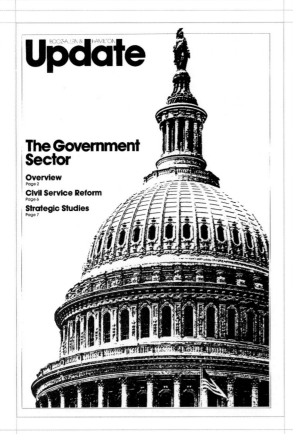

UPDATE

client

BOOZ•ALLEN &
HAMILTON INC.

business

MANAGEMENT
CONSULTING

design firm

SHAPIRO DESIGN
ASSOCIATES INC.

art director/
designer

ELLEN SHAPIRO

illustrator

WALLOP MANYUM

This black-and-white, saddle-stitched newsletter does
not break any new ground,
but within convention gives
the material a strong visual
presence.

pages 6-8, frequency
Bimonthly, quantity 5,000,
software Aldus PageMaker

THE REAL TIME MONITOR

client

SOFTWARE COMPONENTS GROUP

business

SOFTWARE

design firm

SACKETT DESIGN ASSOCIATES

art director

MARK SACKETT

designers

MARK SACKETT
WAYNE SAKAMOTO

This rather conservative saddle-stitched newsletter is mostly type highlighted by a few information graphics. The metallic-ink border on the cover changes each issue.

pages 12, frequency Quarterly, quantity 5,000, software QuarkXPress, Adobe Illustrator

The Real·Time Monitor cover:

SOFTWARE COMPONENTS GROUP

THE REAL·TIME MONITOR

SUMMER '91

A Quarterly Newsletter for SCG Users

THE NEW FACE OF COMMUNICATION

One of my greater regrets of late has been that I am no longer on a first name basis with our more recent customers. This I have come to accept as the price we pay for the company's rapid growth and continued success. With well over two thousand pSOS customers and many more actual users, there is no way I can keep up. But I do miss the old days. And I get a real kick when a long time user, and friend, calls me directly to talk about old or new business, or just to chat about the goings-on in this crazy software business.

So it is with bated breath that I have awaited this premier issue of The Real-Time Monitor. No, the written word is no substitute for one-on-one personal contact. But it does give us an opportunity to reach out and let you get to know us, our products, and our company. One of the common concerns customers have had about Software Components Group has been that we at times failed to keep you up to date on new products, product direction, news from our customers about interesting pSOS applications, and so on. We hear you. This newsletter is just one of several new initiatives to enhance our corporate communication with you, our valued customers.

As for you oldtimers who know me, and newtimers who don't, call me any time. But not, I hope, only when there is a problem.

Warm regards,
—Al

Alfred Chao, President
Software Components Group

INSIDE

Services
p.1-3

Customer Profile
p.4-5

Tech Tips
p.6

International News
p.7

SCG Joins with Intel
p.8

NFS Support
p.9

Growing Up In Real Time
p.10

Products Versions
p.11

News Flash
p.12

Knoll

NETWORK news

The Knoll Group Dealer Newsletter
Volume 1 Issue 1

Chevalier Details "Preeminence" for The Knoll Group Sales and Distribution Team

Robert J. Chevalier, Senior Vice President, Sales and Distribution, better known to most of you as "Bob" or "Chevy", recently challenged his sales and distribution team, to discover their role in building The Knoll Group into the industry leader. Soon after, Knoll Network News staffers caught up with him to find out how this challenge applies to the Dealer-Partner organization.

KNN: Can you tell us briefly what you've asked your sales and distribution team to do?

Chevalier: I've asked them to do quite a number of things, but they can be synthesized into three major objectives: To build a truly superior dealer network, to substantially improve our pricing practices to impact company profitability, and to implement an account planning and management process that begins to build more day-to-day business and brings more discipline and balance to our short-term versus long-term selling focus.

KNN: We're most interested in your plans to build a superior dealer network — please tell us more.

(continued on back cover)

In this Issue
2 Technology Specification
3 Installation Certification
  McKinsey and Company
4 Dealer Advisory Council
  "Heard on the Street"
5 Caliber File
  President's Circle
6 Focus on
  Book Review
7 The Knoll Distribution Group
  New Graphic Standards
8 Angus Reid Survey
  Play Ball!

The Knoll Network News Premiers

Welcome to the premier edition of the Knoll Network News! Published monthly by The Knoll Group Distribution Team, this newsletter is intended to be a platform for dialogue between The Knoll Group and the North American Dealer–Partner Network.

Timing for this kind of a publication seems to be just right. As we all begin to sort through the "how, why and where" of this newly blended organization, questions outnumber obvious answers by a large margin. Each issue of this newsletter will begin to bring you some of those answers with specific,"plain-talk" information on distribution programs, new products, and operational items critical to your business. There will also be regular features about what other Knoll Group Dealer–Partners are doing; what works, what doesn't and what's new. Beyond that, each issue will have a few interesting items about the market or business in general.

The "Network" part of the name here is key. There is an exponential benefit in exploring the questions and answers of this emerging organization, together. Of course, this won't happen in a vacuum, and the Distribution Team won't always have the answers (or perhaps the questions, either), so talk to us. A phone call (212 207.2234) or fax to Sandy Hillmer, Mike Clardy or anyone on The Knoll Group Distribution Team, with your concerns, observations or ideas, is a good place to start the dialogue.

NETWORK NEWS

client

THE KNOLL GROUP

business

FURNITURE

design firm

STUDIO MORRIS

designer

JEFF MORRIS

Knoll is known for its unmistakable corporate design, and this tabloid newsletter is no exception. The bold, though simple, graphic geometries and pastel colors used throughout are consistent with the company's overall identity.

pages 8, frequency Quarterly, quantity 5,000, software QuarkXPress, Adobe Photoshop

hearsay

The official company newsletter of Warner Bros. & Reprise Records

Warner Bros. Gets
Interactive
By Debby Miller

Debut Issue/Spring 1994

They go by such names as America Online, CompuServe, The Well, Prodigy, the Sierra Network and the ominous-sounding *Internet*. They are the interactive computer services, and they have transformed our world.

If you haven't seen them in action, perhaps they're best explained as somewhat akin to magazines, except that their pages are viewed on a computer screen. From these services, subscribers can glean the latest information on a variety of subjects, including world and local news, travel, finance, religion, sports, the entertainment industry, computer software and hardware and a wide array of consumer goods and services. Being interactive, the online services also allow users to communicate with others to share ideas and seek information.

The skinny? Warner Bros. Records is now involved directly with these services. It all began when Warner Bros. employees started subscribing on their own. Our fellow workers were reading the latest gossip on our bands and feeling the need to communicate the truth.

In early 1993, Sire's Ilene Sutter discovered on Prodigy that several fans across the U.S. had obtained bootleg copies of an unreleased Depeche Mode album. After some inspired detective work, she found the sources of the bootlegs and pleaded with those involved to discontinue the copying and selling of them. As a result, people around Ilene's

continued on page 3

Your Burbank Parking Pal. Security officer Howard Washington has been watching the world come and go through Warner's gates for more than six decades.

He Ain't Heavy...He's
Howard
By Alyea Salem

RECENTLY, I HAD THE OPPORTUNITY TO CORNER HOWARD WASHINGTON IN HIS LITTLE GUARD BOOTH AND TALK TO HIM ABOUT HIS LIFE, HIS EARLY DAYS AT WARNER BROS. STUDIOS, AND ANY OTHER TOPIC THAT CAME TO MIND.

Though I've only worked at Warner Bros. Records a little over two years, I feel lucky to have gotten acquainted with this remarkable man. Howard is a truly unique individual, still going strong at 84 years young. He has worked at Warner Bros. for over 64 years and has rubbed shoulders with the likes of James Dean, Humphrey Bogart, James Cagney, Errol Flynn and Joan Crawford. If that weren't enough, Howard has appeared as an extra in over 100 Warner Bros. Films, including a speaking role in Alfred Hitchcock's *Strangers On A Train*, in which Howard played the part of the porter.

If I had more time, I'm sure I could fill volumes of books with the adventures of Howard, but instead, I thought it would be fun to ask Howard a few questions about himself, his life, his career, women, the movies and, of course, the music business.

continued on page 2

HEARSAY

client
WARNER BROS. RECORDS

business
RECORD COMPANY

design firm
WARNER BROS. RECORDS

art directors/ designers
JERI HEIDEN
STINE SCHYBERG

This cluttered, but eye-catching two-color newsletter makes optimum use of color bars and tints to draw the eye in various directions.

pages 8, frequency Bimonthly, software QuarkXPress

DIRECTIONS

client
AMERICAN-STANDARD

business
HOME PRODUCTS

design firm
THE BARNETT GROUP

art directors
DAVID BARNETT
THEO FELS

designer
DAVID BARNETT

This two-color newsletter avoids black entirely. The harmonious type and image integration makes this otherwise stodgy business news very accessible.

pages 4, frequency Quarterly, quantity 15,000, software Quark XPress, Aldus Freehand, Adobe Photoshop

---

A newsletter to aid in the successful implementation of demand flow processes worldwide by providing information and ideas to American-Standard employees

january

volume 1 No. 1

directions

CHARTING A COURSE FOR EXCELLENCE

design for success

welcome to the first issue of the new *Directions* newsletter. In these pages, you will find a mix of Demand Flow Technology news, information, helpful tips and guidelines.

Nearly four years ago, American-Standard embarked upon a challenging mission to become a world-class manufacturer. What does it mean to be a "world-class" manufacturer? It means manufacturing products that meet the highest standards of performance and quality at competitive prices, getting our products to market faster than our competitors, and passionately serving our customers. Demand Flow Technology is the business strategy adopted by our company to help us accomplish that mission. This exacting technology has already proven that it is possible to manufacture high-quality products with available resources at a faster pace. Our successes in implementing DFT are many, but we can do more.

The potential for DFT to thoroughly transform our company is enormous. That transformation will result in productivity gains, profit and inventory improvement, reduced cycle times, faster product introductions, higher quality products and more satisfied customers. It will also mean a more flexible, stronger, growth-oriented American-Standard. *Directions* is devoted to tracking our corporate transformation toward performance excellence through DFT. It is a great deal of ground to cover, and we will need your help. We want to know how you are doing. Feel free to share your mistakes and success stories.

Any comments or suggestions you may have in making *Directions* more valuable to you are welcome. Until next month.

CYRIL GALLIMORE EDITOR

LISA GLOVER MANAGING EDITOR

world-class manufacturer

Fashioning Mixed Model Flow Line with Simultaneous Engineering

PENANG, MALAYSIA - If given six months, could you develop a flow line to manufacture a product in six different sizes? In March of this year, Trane Malaysia faced that challenge. The facility had to create a flow line to produce self-contained unitary cooling units (SWUQ) ranging in size from 7.5 to 60 ton capacity.

From the beginning, the success of the project hinged on the involvement of several different departments. Trane Malaysia marshalled the collective know-how of staff members from the customer service, design, drafting, facilities, manufacturing engineering, marketing, materials, production, purchasing, quality and tooling departments. C.L. Ho, engineering manager, led the 20-member Unitary DFM team.

A role for everyone > The DFM team formed three subgroups to tackle the project - the Materials Group, the Process Group and the Design Group. Each group had distinct responsibilities. The Design and Process Groups worked closely together to match the design and technical specifications of SWUQ. They determined the flow of the skin and frame cells supplying the production line. Additionally, production team members within the Design Group worked with manufacturing engineers from the Process Group to fabricate the prototype parts in

Penang, Malaysia

[*continued on page 2*]

Michael Stanard, Inc.
996 Main Street
Evanston, Illinois 60202

S T A N ⊘ A R D

UP YOUR STANARD

client

MICHAEL STANARD, INC.

business

GRAPHIC DESIGN

design firm

MICHAEL STANARD, INC.

art director/
designer

MICHAEL STANARD

As its title suggests, this newsletter is playful—yet serious. The purposeful visual clutter is at once a maze of images and a sampler of the designer's quarterly output.

pages 8, frequency Quarterly, quantity 5,000, software QuarkXPress

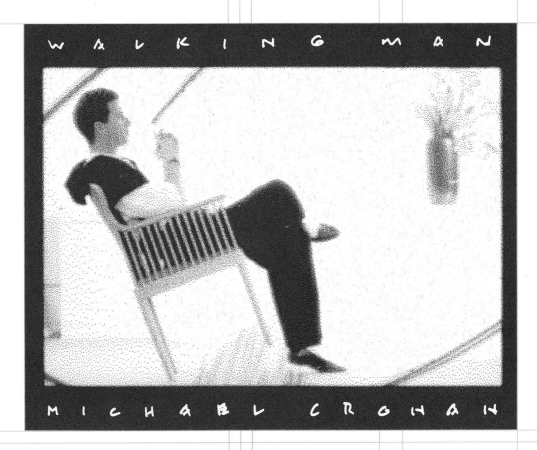

W/M

client

CRONAN ARTEFACT

business

PRODUCT DEVELOPMENT/ PROMOTION

design firm

CRONAN DESIGN

art director/ designer

MICHAEL CRONAN

photographer

TERRY LORANT

To promote Walking Man clothes and the business's personality, this quirky newsletter is part catalog and part gossip sheet. Its free-form and playful design is enhanced by the rich black-and-white printing.

pages 6, frequency Biannually, quantity 10,000, software QuarkXPress

SERIOUS FUN!

client

LINCOLN CENTER PRODUCTIONS

business

PERFORMING ARTS CENTER

design firm

HARP AND COMPANY

art director

DOUGLAS HARP

designers

DOUGLAS HARP LINDA E. WAGNER

This web offset newsletter uses one big collage for the illustration. The effect is posterlike; it underscores the title and befits a major cultural institution.

pages 16, frequency Annually, quantity 150,000, software Aldus PageMaker

FUN!

I.E.

client

TIME WARNER, INC.

business

MEDIA AND ENTERTAINMENT

design firm

WBMG

art director

JESSICA SIMMONS

designers

MICHAEL GROSSMAN WALTER BERNARD MILTON GLASER

illustrator

TIM LEWIS

A lot of information is handsomely and efficiently crammed into this format, and still there is room for a dedicated cover and smart conceptual illustrations.

pages 16, frequency Monthly, quantity 48,000, software QuarkXPress

Neo-CEOs • Big Shoes & Baby Steps • A Giant Texan

ic

i.e. INFORMATION ENTERTAINMENT

GLOBULLISH

Time Warner Sees a Shrinking Planet and a Growing Market

TIME WARNER
SEPTEMBER 1990

TCR TIMES COMPANY REPORT

client

THE NEW YORK TIMES COMPANY

business

COMMUNICATIONS

design firm

TANA & CO.

art director/ designer

TANA KAMINE

illustrator

GENE GREIF

This four-color magazine-style quarterly printed on glossy stock is contemporary in its generous use of white space, fashionable, often widely leaded typography, and decorative/conceptual illustrations sprinkled throughout the formal color photography.

pages 16, frequency Quarterly, quantity 15,000, software QuarkXPress, Adobe Illustrator

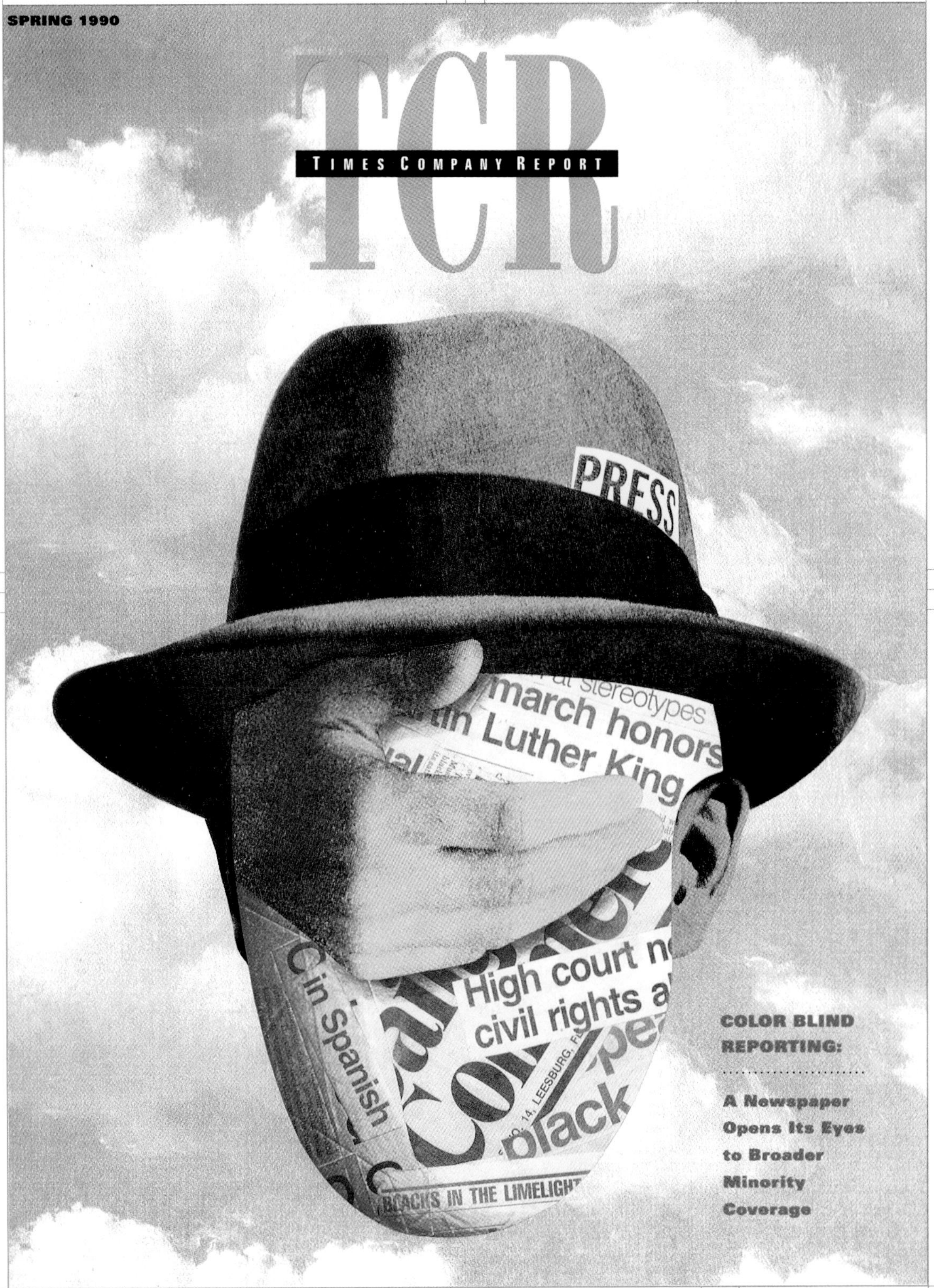

SPRING 1990
TCR
TIMES COMPANY REPORT
PRESS
stereotypes
march honors
Luther King
High court n
civil rights a
in Spanish
black
BLACKS IN THE LIMELIGHT
COLOR BLIND REPORTING:
A Newspaper Opens Its Eyes to Broader Minority Coverage

JAKE'S NOTES
client

JAKE'S ATTIC
business

CHILDREN'S TV SHOW
design firm

GRETEMAN GROUP
art director

SONIA GRETEMAN
designer/ illustrator

GRETEMAN GROUP

The visuals for this four-color newsletter are all conceptual illustrations that are smartly integrated with the typography.

pages 4, frequency Biannually, quantity 5,000, software Aldus PageMaker

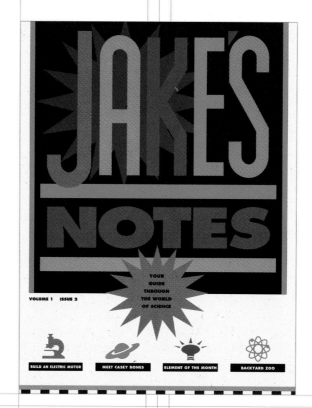

JAKE'S NOTES

YOUR GUIDE THROUGH THE WORLD OF SCIENCE

VOLUME 1 ISSUE 2

BUILD AN ELECTRIC MOTOR · MEET CASEY BONES · ELEMENT OF THE MONTH · BACKYARD ZOO

SPARK YOUR IMAGINATION

EXPERIMENT ONE

JAKE'S EASY TO BUILD ELECTRIC MOTOR

DESCRIPTION: In three or four minutes, you can construct a very simple electric motor.

YOU WILL NEED: A thick rubber band, two paper clips, a 1.5 volt "D" cell, a small disc-shaped magnet, a few inches of wire (#22 gauge, non-insulated, varnish coated wire works well. It can be obtained at a radio or hardware store).

HERE'S HOW:

1. To make the rotating part of the motor (the field coil), coil ten turns of the #22 wire, leaving a slight hook on the long ends, as shown in the illustration.

2. Scrape the varnish off of the top half of the two wire ends.

3. As shown, use the two paper clips to form supports for the coil.

4. Use the rubber band to hold the coil supports at the ends of the D cell.

5. Secure the magnet with tape or glue to the middle of the cell.

6. Place the coil in the supports and give the coil a gentle "flick."

The coil will rotate — you have built an electric motor.

EXPERIMENT 2

SEWER LEECHES

DESCRIPTION: With a little knowledge of science, you can make a colony of imaginary creatures that will amaze and fool your friends.

YOU WILL NEED: A tall, narrow glass container, clear, carbonated soft drink or club soda, a few raisins, and a dark piece of cloth.

HERE'S HOW:

1. Wash and rinse the glass thoroughly.

2. Slowly fill the glass with the soft drink. Try to avoid making foam.

3. Carefully drop in a few raisins.

4. At first, the raisins will sink. Eventually, they will "swim" to the surface and return to the bottom of the cylinder. They will repeat the cycle for several minutes.

5. Cover the glass with the cloth. Remove it when you show your colony of sewer leeches to your friends. Explain that the creatures don't like bright light. You can even capture one of the creatures and eat it!

WHAT'S HAPPENING: The soft drink contains a gas called carbon dioxide, or CO_2. Bubbles of the gas collect on the sides of the raisins. Eventually, there will be enough bubbles on the raisins to make it float to the surface. Some of the bubbles will break at the surface and the raisin will sink to the bottom. From a distance, the raisins actually look like small creatures swimming in the liquid.

THE CHALLENGE: Develop as many explanations as you can about your imaginary creatures.

WHERE DID YOU CAPTURE THEM? WHAT DO YOU FEED THEM? WHY DON'T THEY LIKE THE LIGHT?

You might be able to fool your friends for only a few minutes, but it is some good science fun to try!

FACTOIDS

The **RED SKY** seen at sunrise and sunset is caused by the scattering of light. Sunlight is a mixture of many different colors of light. The short waves of blue light are scattered by dust particles in the air. Red light has a longer wavelength and is able to pass through the dusty air.

The white halo sometimes seen around the **MOON** is caused by tiny ice crystals in the upper atmosphere.

The average **RAINBOW** lasts about 7 minutes.

Backyard ZOO

PRAYING MANTIS: The praying mantis is one of the few insects that is valued by man. It is valuable because it eats many other harmful insects.

The mantis gets its name from the position of its front legs. The legs are equipped with spikes used to hold its food. The mantis has very powerful jaws, but is harmless to humans.

HOUSING THE PRAYING MANTIS: You can keep the mantis in a large jar with holes punched in the lid, or a small aquarium with a screen over the top. The mantis needs room to move around.

Place sand or soil in the bottom of the jar. Provide some branches for climbing. Include a shallow dish or jar lid with water and a stone to hold it in place. You may need to place the jar near a 25w light bulb to provide heat. Try to maintain the same temperature and humidity as the location where you found the mantis. The mantis will not survive cold temperatures.

DIET: The mantis will eat live crickets and other small insects. They will even capture houseflies.

Element OF THE MONTH

CARBON What do diamonds, pencil lead and charcoal have in common? They are all made of carbon. Carbon reacts so easily with other elements that over 1 million carbon compounds are known to exist; such as carbon dioxide, gasoline, nylon, sugar, cellulose (paper), and natural gas.

EXPERIMENT 3

BENDING A STREAM OF WATER

DESCRIPTION: You can mysteriously bend a stream of running water, without touching it!

YOU WILL NEED: A plastic comb, an inflated balloon, a piece of dry cloth, (wool works well) and the kitchen sink.

HERE'S HOW:

1. Turn on the cold water and adjust the flow until it is very fine, about the size of the lead in a pencil.

2. Brush your hair with the plastic comb and bring the comb near the stream of water. Do not touch the water with the comb.

3. The stream of water will bend towards the comb.

WHAT'S HAPPENING: Pulling the comb through your hair creates a charge of static electricity on the comb. The field created around the comb causes an opposite charge to be created in the stream of water. The opposite charges are attracted to each other and the water moves towards the comb.

THE CHALLENGE: Try using different items, such as stroking the balloon with the cloth, to create a static charge and see if it will affect the stream of water. How about a ruler or piece of plastic sandwich wrap?

Casey Bones SAYS

HABITAT

HAB = living

TAT = site

The place that a plant or animal normally lives and grows is called its habitat. The habitat for a fish is _?_ ... for a cactus is _?_ ... for an owl is _?_.

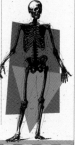

DISCOVER

client

HALLMARK/CREATIVE RESOURCE DIVISION

business

GREETING CARDS

design firm

SACKETT DESIGN ASSOCIATES

art director

MARK SACKETT

designers

MARK SACKETT WAYNE SAKAMOTO

photographer

JERI GLEITER

This full-color publication makes lively use of its well paced articles and news-briefs. The so-called candid photos are not used large but rather as welcome accents.

pages 24, frequency Quarterly, quantity 5,000, software QuarkXPress, Adobe Illustrator

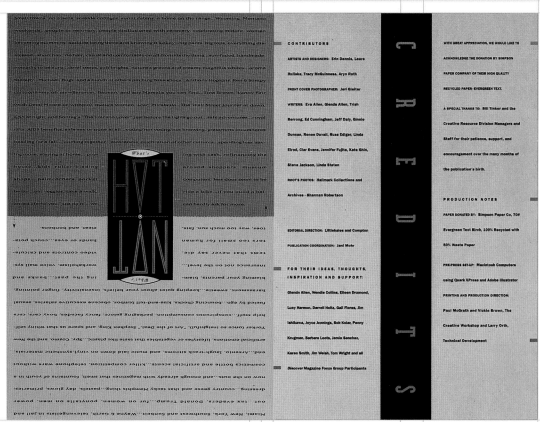

ingenuity.

BRAZOS MALL & OSHMAN'S
A SUCCESS

KILLEEN MALL STRONG SALES

TEMPLE MALL'S NEW
FOOD COURT

PECANLAND MALL & THE
LIMITED LEADING THE WAY

ALEXANDRIA MALL OPENING
EXPRESS / STRUCTURE

MARATHON 6% SALES
INCREASE

NEW MEXICO PROPERTIES
CONTINUE SOLID GROWTH

PARK PLAZA COMMUNITY
PROGRAMS WIN MAXI

MARATHON
Shopping Centers Group

19
92

M

client
MARATHON SHOPPING
CENTERS GROUP

business
SHOPPING CENTERS

design firm
BRAINSTORM, INC.

art directors/
designers
CHUCK JOHNSON
TOM VASQUEZ

illustrators
CHUCK JOHNSON
TOM VASQUEZ

photographers
NEILL WHITLOCK
BEN BRITT
DAN BRYANT

Continued on pages 132 and 133.

i n g

It is a skill or cleverness in creating or planning. In the world of retail, ingenuity describes Marathon. With the experience, talent and desire to create productive retail opportunities across North America, we combine innovative problem solving with financial stability to initiate growth for our retailers. At Marathon, we utilize a novel business approach that establishes our retailers as partners. And we devote ourselves to "Service Excellence" as a means to an improved bottom line. If you want ingenuity that's a step ahead of the rest, join us at our booth at 5-J St. at the ICSC Convention, May 12-14.

WHEN DEVELOPER AND RETAILER WORK TOGETHER, SUCCESS IS THE SURE RESULT. AT BRAZOS MALL IN LAKE JACKSON, TEXAS THE LONG AWAITED COMPANY'S SUPERSTORE HAS BEEN DOING TWICE THE SALES STORE OFFICIALS HAD PROJECTED. PRE-OPENING EXPOSURE WAS THE KEY HERE, INCLUDING IN-STORE PREVIEW PARTIES HELD FOR BOTH MALL MERCHANTS AND AREA BUSINESS AND CIVIC OFFICIALS.

compatibility.

credibility.

BILLED MALL IN KILLEEN, TEXAS HAS SURVIVED THE GULF CRISIS AND ITS STABILITY-BASED MARKET IS STRONGER THAN EVER. SALES INCREASES HAVE CONTINUED TO SHOW IN DOUBLE DIGITS SINCE THE RETURN OF THE TROOPS. WITH THE 5TH MECHANIZED INFANTRY DIVISION FROM FORT POLK, LOUISIANA SOON TO BE STATIONED HERE, AN ADDITIONAL 12,800 TROOPS WILL BE ADDED TO THE CUSTOMER BASE. IN ADDITION, NEARBY TEMPLE MALL (ALSO OWNED BY MARATHON) AND ITS NEW FOOD COURT CREATE AN OPPORTUNITY FOR RETAILERS TO CASH IN ON THE MARATHON STRONGHOLD OF THE TEXAS CENTROPLEX.

---

i n g e n u i t y.

It is a skill or cleverness in creating or planning. In the world of retail, ingenuity describes Marathon. With the experience, talent and desire to create productive retail opportunities across North America, we combine innovative problem solving with financial stability to initiate growth for our retailers. At Marathon, we utilize a novel business approach that establishes our retailers as partners. And we devote ourselves to "Service Excellence" as a means to an improved bottom line. If you want ingenuity that's a step ahead of the rest, join us at our booth at 5-J St. at the ICSC Convention, May 12-14.

fashionability.

impactibility.

profitability.

creativity.

SALES AT THE MARATHON NEW MEXICO PROPERTIES ARE SURE TO CONTINUE WITH THIS SOLID GROWTH MARKET. AMERICAN DEMOGRAPHICS RECENTLY CITED THIS SOUTHWESTERN STATE AS ONE OF FEW PREDICTED TO HAVE INCREASING AVERAGE HOUSEHOLD INCOMES. MERCHANDISE-SPECIFIC SALES PROGRAMS HERE ARE AIMED AT CAPTURING DISPOSABLE DOLLARS. AT A FALL TOY FAIR AT MESILLA VALLEY MALL, MANUFACTURERS SHOWCASED THEIR NEWEST TOY PRODUCTS. THIS PRE-HOLIDAY EVENT GARNERED THOUSANDS OF DOLLARS IN SALES GAINS FOR TOY, MUSIC AND ELECTRONICS RETAILERS.

WITH A 89% COMPARABLE SALES INCREASE OF 5% COMPANY-WIDE, MARATHON PROVES ITS COMMITMENT TO RESULTS. THIS PARTNERSHIP TOWARD PROFITABILITY IS AIMED AT MAKING AN IMPACT WHERE IT MATTERS MOST - AT THE BOTTOM LINE.

PARK PLAZA & COMMUNITY PROGRAMS CONTINUE TO BE A AGARD-WINNING WITH A RECENT MAXI MERIT AWARD. THE POWER OF THESE LOYALTY BUILDING PROGRAMS CONTINUE TO SHOW AT THE BOTTOM LINE IN THE LITTLE ROCK, ARKANSAS MALL. SALES OF LIFESTYLE MERCHANTS SOARED HERE, INCLUDING THE GAP, WHO RECENTLY HIT THE $500 PER SQ. FT. MARK.

As a fashion statement this newsletter takes the runway prize. The clever application of two-, three-, and four-color printing makes this a lively testament to its primary theme.

pages 6, frequency Annually, quantity 5,000, software QuarkXPress, Adobe Illustrator, Adobe Photoshop

BRAZOS MALL RECYCLING PROGRAM A SUCCESS!

Villa Linda Mall

to open a new

Waldenbooks super

store & Western

Warehouse

BRAND NEW & EXCITING!

Alexandria Mall's

super growth with

Oshman's SuperSports

The Power of

Marathon's Customer

Service Philosophy

Park Plaza will

bring shoppers the

very latest with new

GAP/GAP Kids &

Banana Republic

MARATHON
Shopping Centers Group

GFYI

client

GENERAL FOODS USA

business

CONSUMER

design firm

THE BARNETT GROUP, INC.

art directors

DAVID BARNETT
THEO FELS
LISA BERNICH

designer

LISA BERNICH

illustrator

JULIA GORTON

To give employees pride in their company, this four-color tabloid is handsomely designed to show that management cares. The illustrations and photographs complement each other nicely; this is not just another generic corporate publication, but a well-planned document.

pages 4, frequency Quarterly, quantity 25,000 (Printed in 6 languages), software QuarkXPress

WORLDVIEW

client

DUN & BRADSTREET

business

CREDIT CLEARING HOUSE

design firm

THE BARNETT GROUP, INC.

art directors

THEO FELS
DAVID BARNETT

designer

THEO FELS

This four-color newsprint broadsheet begins four stories on the front, along with a lively news summary. The illustrations are used smartly as complements to the text.

pages 6-10, frequency Bimonthly, quantity 60,000 (Printed in 7 languages), software QuarkXPress, Adobe Photoshop

THE evolution OF new services

We will now discuss in a little more detail the struggle for existence.

—CHARLES DARWIN (1809–1882)

insidetrack

Special Issue May 1994

LEARN FROM THE BEST

BENCHMARKING HELPS CLIENTS

(Continued on page 6)

(Continued on page 6)

INSIDE TRACK 1994

client
KPMG PEAT MARWICK

business
ACCOUNTING

design firm
THE BARNETT GROUP, INC.

art director/designer
DAVID BARNETT

illustrator
COCO MATSUDA

photographer
MARY ANN CARTER/MERCURY

The annual report format is effectively used here. Fine conceptual illustration and illustrative information graphics are employed.

pages Varies, frequency Monthly, quantity 40,000, software QuarkXPress, Adobe Photoshop

---

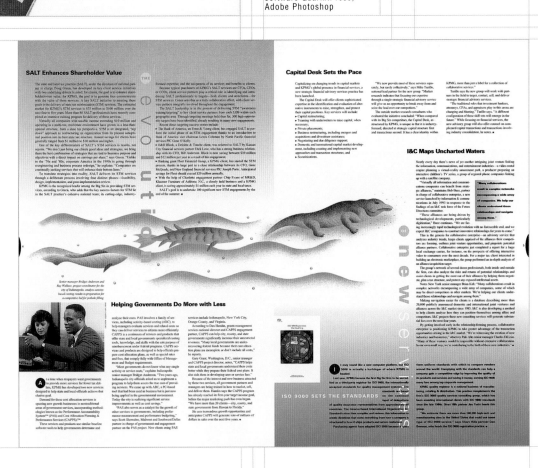

SALT Enhances Shareholder Value

Capital Desk Sets the Pace

I&C Maps Uncharted Waters

Helping Governments Do More with Less

ISO 9000 SETS THE STANDARDS

STEP-BY-STEP ELECTRONIC DESIGN

client

STEP-BY-STEP PUBLISHING, DIVISION OF DYNAMIC GRAPHICS, INC.

business

PUBLISHING

design firm

STEP-BY-STEP PUBLISHING

art director

MICHAEL ULRICH

illustrator

TOM WARD

This four-color newsletter complements *Step-By-Step Graphics*, the bimonthly how-to magazine. This provides hands-on information, designed and illustrated in a no-nonsense manner. Unlike the magazine, it does not use lavish studio photography.

pages 16, frequency Monthly, quantity 21,000, software Microsoft Word, QuarkXPress, Aldus Freehand, Adobe Illustrator, Adobe Photoshop, Exposure Pro

STEP·BY·STEP
Electronic Design

THE HOW-TO NEWSLETTER   MARCH 1994 VOLUME 6, NUMBER 3   SIX DOLLARS U.S.

FREEHAND / PHOTOSHOP

Capturing Rich, Painterly Texture

■ *by Sara Booth*

OR MOST ARTISTS, the color shift that occurs in the transition between 24-bit and 8-bit color is a nuisance. For Long Beach, Calif., illustrator Tom Ward, it's the beginning of an artistic technique. Ward creates an image in Aldus FreeHand, rotates it, then sets his monitor for 8-bit color and takes a screen capture. This screen capture is rotated back into a vertical position in Adobe Photoshop and then manipulated slightly before being recombined with some of the elements of the original PostScript image. It's a process that takes advantage of the way monitors dither images on screen to simulate colors they can't represent accurately, and the result is a surprising combination of crisp lines and painterly textures.

Ward begins with a pencil sketch. If he feels he must be faithful to his initial sketch, he scans it, then traces the scan in FreeHand. In this case, though, he felt free to make changes as he went along. So he used his pencil sketch as a reference and redrew the design with the freehand tool ❶. He prefers the freehand tool for linework. "You get more accidents, more little unpredictable jags and wiggles."

LAYERING THE ILLUSTRATION
Ward worked in three layers. He had drawn the computer sketch on FreeHand's default Foreground layer. To create a background layer, he opened the Layers palette (accessed through the Windows menu in FreeHand 4.0 and in the View, Windows submenu in earlier versions). Then he selected New from the palette's pop-out menu and named the layer *Back*. FreeHand automatically places new layers on top, and the layering sequence is reflected in the order of names listed in the palette. Ward rearranged the

Tom Ward took advantage of the way monitors dither images to simulate colors they can't represent and used the dithering to add painterly texture to this illustration. After creating a PostScript design, he set his monitor to 8-bit color display to exaggerate the on-screen dithering, took a screen capture, and manipulated the screen capture in Photoshop.

HOME FRONT

client

PRUDENTIAL HOME MORTGAGE

business

MORTGAGE

design firm

PATTERSON WOOD PARTNERS

art director/ designer

PEG PATTERSON

illustrator

MICHAEL KLEIN

The same kind of conceptual illustration is used on each and every cover. The lead story begins, or is announced, on the cover and continues inside. The interior layouts are low key, but not uninteresting.

pages 4, frequency Quarterly, quantity 2,000, software QuarkXPress

News, Views and Insights from Prudential Home Mortgage

HOME *front*

October 1994

MODIFYING MORTGAGE ASSISTANCE
to Match the Market

daptability has become the watchword of corporate life in the nineties. Flex-time, telecommuting, job sharing and re-engineering are all trends that have sprung up to help us adapt to changes in our culture, lifestyle and economy. One of the newest trends on the corporate landscape is a movement to develop mortgage assistance programs that can readily adapt to changes in interest rates, while maximizing the benefit to employees.

Back in the early eighties, companies reacted to rising interest rates by reimbursing as many as three to four points to help cover the cost of additional discount points or interest rate buy-downs. But now that interest rates are no longer in double digits, some companies have moved away from programs with fixed point reimbursement, and toward more fluid plans that can adapt to the changing market.

In Favor of Flexibility
"Some companies decided to reduce their point reimbursement given the low rate environment, but just as they started to do that, interest rates started to head up again," says Deborah Silvan, a marketing director at Prudential Home Mortgage. "I encourage my clients to build flexibility into their programs, so assistance can increase with rising interest rates, when it's needed most."

The desire for this kind of flexibility has led to the development of a sliding scale policy, which bases the number of discount points paid by the company on the current interest rate. Prudential Home Mortgage is seeing more clients express interest in a sliding scale concept.

UPS in Atlanta, Ga., is one company that changed its policy to a sliding scale last November with the help of Prudential Home Mortgage. Since UPS relocates approximately 1,000 homeowners annually, Jim White, corporate relocation manager at UPS, believes the savings will be substantial. White estimates that UPS could save more than $500,000 this year, depending on interest rates and the value of homes purchased.

Smart Spending
Another alternative is reallocating the assistance. Companies can increase the benefit received by employees without increasing their investment, by shortening the length of time over which the assistance is paid.

"The average transferee doesn't stay in his/her home long enough to recoup the full benefit of a permanent discount point program," says Michael Sperazza, also a marketing director at Prudential Home Mortgage. "Most companies distribute funds over the full term of the mortgage — 15 or 30 years — and yet transferees relocate every three to seven years on average."

For that reason, companies are implementing shorter term subsidies, where the full
continued on page four

Prudential Home Mortgage

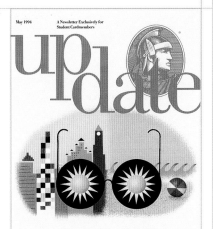

May 1994 — A Newsletter Exclusively for Student Cardmembers

update

American Express: A Card for All Seasons

Whether your summer plans involve backpacking around Bali or—more likely—putting in some hard time in an office with no windows and too much air-conditioning, you can continue to depend on the American Express® Card to offer you services and benefits throughout the summer.

If you are relocating from the area where you go to school, you can rely on more than 1,700 American Express Travel Service locations worldwide* to help you once you arrive at your destination. To find the Travel Service location nearest you, call 800-528-4800.

Once you've relocated, at most Travel Service locations you can:

Cash your personal checks.

Send or receive American Express MoneyGrams (at those Travel Service Offices with MoneyGram locations.)

If you're lucky enough to take off traveling this summer, you'll find that the Card can also be a link to home in an emergency; simply call the Global Assist℠ Hotline at 800-554-AMEX from within the U.S.; in Washington, D.C., or if you are abroad, call 202-554-2639 collect.

Global Assist will:

Deliver an important message home.

Give you local medical or legal referrals or help locate a replacement prescription you may have forgotten to pack.

When on the road, go to a Travel Service location to:

Obtain emergency cash, a replacement Card, or Travelers Cheques if your wallet is lost or stolen.

Exchange foreign currency.

Purchase American Express® Travelers Cheques (available in seven currencies).

Wherever you choose to spend the next few months, American Express, as always, can provide the financial services and travel security you'll need to make your summer a breeze.

Corporate Travel Service locations of American Express Travel Related Service Company, Inc., its affiliates, and Representatives worldwide. All dedicated services are subject to local laws and regulations. Not all services are available at all locations.

Remember to watch for the July issue of Update:

Its cover art will be the winning entry in the competition announced in the March issue. Aspiring student illustrators were invited to give artistic expression to their ideas about summer. The winner will also receive $500 in American Express® Gift Cheques.

?

UPDATE

client

AMERICAN EXPRESS TRAVEL RELATED SERVICES CO., INC.

business

CHARGE CARD

design firm

DONOVAN AND GREEN

design director

MARGE LEVIN

designer

PAUL CARLOS

illustrators

TERRY ALLEN *(left)*
BRIAN CRONIN *(bottom left)*
JOSE ORTEGA *(bottom right)*

Today a charge card is the student's coin of the realm. This unique American Express newsletter is designed to appeal to the young creditor with stylish illustration and accessible graphics.

pages 3, software QuarkXPress, Adobe Illustrator, Adobe Photoshop

---

March 1994 — A Newsletter Exclusively for Student Cardmembers

update

How Much Do *You* Know About Finances?

If you answered the quiz correctly, then congratulations—you have reached a higher degree of financial literacy than the average college student. A recent survey, cosponsored by the Consumer Federation of America and the American Express Company, showed that students tested knew only half of the answers to questions about financial services offered to them.

The results of the survey, which was conducted on 75 campuses throughout the country, show that students could do better when it comes to consumer finance. For example, while 92% realized that a good bill-paying history is the best route to getting a loan, only 37% knew the difference between a charge and a credit card. And only 30% were

QUICK QUIZ:

A) Are bill-paying records and income more important than education and occupation when loan applications are reviewed?

B) How do credit cards differ from charge cards?

C) When do interest charges begin accruing on new credit purchases if a balance is carried from the previous month?

(A) The most important factors in determining whether to make a loan are bill-paying history and income.

(B) You pay interest on a credit card, whereas you pay a charge card in full each month.

(C) You'll start paying interest on the day of the new purchase.

aware that, on a credit-card account, if you carry over a balance from the previous month, you start paying interest charges on any new purchases from the day of purchase. Normally, you are granted a 3-4 week grace period if you pay off all your previous charges.

The survey teaches an important lesson: It's not just practicing financial responsibility. **To help you become a more informed consumer, American Express has compiled *A Plain English Dictionary of Credit Terms* (call 800-528-4800 for your free copy).**

Big News Win $500 in American Express® Gift Cheques

Your work can win $500. That's the prize for the illustration selected for publication on the cover of the July 1994 issue of *Update*. You may request an entry form and contest guidelines by writing to "Student Illustration Contest," 71 Fifth Avenue, 4th floor, New York, NY 10003; by faxing to 212-989-1453; or by calling 800-582-5823. Be sure to share this Big News with your friends.

September 1994 — A Newsletter Exclusively for Student Cardmembers

update

Get Going! with the 1994-95 Travel Program

The Student Travel Certificates you receive every year are a very important part of Student Cardmembership, enabling you to travel home for an emergency, visit family and friends, take that honeymoon, or just get away from it all. That's why American Express and Continental Airlines have been working hard to make your travel benefits even better.

Here are details about the next set of travel certificates you'll be receiving in October: You'll receive five certificates—four for domestic travel to anywhere Continental or Continental Express flies within the 48 contiguous United States) and one for international travel.

1,2,3 With the first three "Mississippi Divide Certificates," you can purchase a round-trip Coach Class ticket for $159 for travel contained either east or west of the Mississippi River ($239 if you cross the Mississippi). Restricted travel dates apply to these three certificates: you may not use them for travel to/from Florida between February 12 and April 30, 1995, and between June 15 and August 25, 1995.

4 The fourth certificate, the "Florida Sun Saver Certificate," is valid for round-trip Coach Class travel to/from Florida between February 12 and April 30, 1995,

and between June 15 and August 25, 1995. It gives you the great fare of $239 between Florida and points east of the Mississippi (or $299 for travel between Florida and points west of the Mississippi).

5 The fifth certificate gives you $50 off an international round trip Coach-b Class fare of $100-$599, or $75 off an international round-trip fare of $600 or more.

If you're traveling with a friend, you may purchase his or her ticket with yours for the same low fare, as long as the payment is charged to your American Express account.

Reservations for domestic travel must be made and the tickets charged to your American Express account within 21 days of travel. A maximum stay of 14 days is allowed. Your stay must include at least one Saturday night. *Complete terms and conditions for all the travel offers will be included on your certificates, which will be sent to you in October.*

As an added benefit, new OnePass enrollees will receive 1,500 bonus miles. Existing Student Cardmembers who are already enrolled in OnePass can receive 1,000 extra OnePass bonus miles. *To enroll in OnePass and receive bonus miles, just complete the enrollment form in your package.*

It's the Season: Writers Harvest 1994

If it's fall, it must be time for harvest—the harvest, that is. This national event, which takes place on **Wednesday, November 2, 1994,** is organized by the national hunger-relief organization Share Our Strength (SOS) and sponsored nationally for the third year by American Express. This literary benefit for hunger relief in the U.S. will bring together writers and poets to read from their work at campuses, libraries, coffee shops, and bookstores in more than 200 locations across the country. Proceeds from the event will be distributed to fight hunger in the U.S. **To get involved with the Writers Harvest, or for more information on how you can help fight hunger, call SOS at 800-955-8278.**

VISION

client

**AMERITECH
CORPORATION**

business

TELECOMMUNICATIONS

design firm

**CROSBY ASSOCIATES
INC.**

art director

BART CROSBY

designers

**JAN GULLY
ANGELA NORWOOD
BART CROSBY**

photographer

**JOHN SOBCZAK/LORIEN
STUDIO**

The most noteworthy aspect
of this handsomely designed
newsletter is the boxed
referral lines under the logo
which indicate that this
piece is replete with interesting content.

pages 8, frequency Monthly,
quantity 70,000, software
QuarkXPress

LATTISNEWS

client

**SYNOPTICS
COMMUNICATIONS, INC.**

business

**TELECOMMUNICATIONS
ADVANCED
TECHNOLOGY**

design firm

**COLEMAN SOUTER
DESIGN**

art director

MARK COLEMAN

designers

**ERIK WATTS
KRISTINA LAMOUR**

Large type is not the only
element of this newsletter
on a grand scale. The striking four-color graphics give
this a posterlike character.

pages 8, frequency
Quarterly, quantity 5,000,
software QuarkXPress,
Adobe Photoshop

Some interesting people make up Saturn's sales team.

Police Chief Marcel Jojola nabs attention in his new patrol car.

Three-on-three basketball challenge and test drives.

Saturn sedan beats out Mazda, Nissan, and Honda for Best small car.

VISIONS

⊼ SATURN Published for Saturn Team Members and their families.   June/July 1992

Saturn on Two Wheels

Saturn will take to the track on two wheels instead of four when the 13-man, all-American amateur cycling team sponsored by Saturn competes in more than 50 races on the U.S. national circuit throughout 1992.

During the year, twenty races will be highlighted for special promotion, complete with four white Saturn pace cars decked out in Saturn logos, booths for Saturn displays and media coverage.

"We have been looking for an event to sponsor for the last two years," says Sales, Service and Marketing Vice President Don Hudler. Saturn surveyed a vast number of opportunities for corporate affiliations and events marketing. Basically, events marketing is a way for a corporation to reach its target market through sponsorship or association with sports teams, cultural activities or organizations. These associations extend the company's advertising message beyond the traditional media.

"We didn't want to get into costly, overused sports like tennis or golf," Hudler says. "Hal Riney & Partners, our advertising agency, recommended cycling as a perfect match for us."

Bicycling enthusiasts and members of Saturn's target market are extremely similar. Bicycling is the largest growing form of recreation within Saturn's target audience. "Cycling represents good family fun. It's healthy, positive and something everyone can relate to. And it's something our retailers can tie into locally. It's a natural. And no other car company has a commercial involvement with cycling," Hudler says. "We're very excited. This will be another extension of Saturn's uniqueness."

All 13 members of Team Saturn, as they are known, are Category One racers and are among the top 250 ranked cyclists in the nation. Team Saturn racers Bob Mionske and Matt Hamon will represent the U.S. in this summer's Olympic Games in Barcelona, Spain. Scott Fortner and Chann McRae have made the team as alternates.

"Cycling is also a perfect fit for Saturn values because you win as a team, not as an individual," Hudler says.

Team Saturn Coach Warren Gibson says, "We've worked very long and hard to put the right chemistry together and have the right guys that will blend together well and work as a team. To do well in cycling you have to ride well as a team. That enhances each guy's individual performance as well as the team's performance."

In keeping with Saturn's values and philosophy, Team Saturn will evolve into both a men's and women's cycling team. Hudler says, "This year, we hope to simply gain experience and establish Saturn's association with cycling. We want to see if cycling does what we think it will—if we're even close, it will be a home run for Saturn."

Team Saturn places 1st and 3rd at Cat's Hill Criterium, Los Gatos, California.

VISIONS

client

SATURN CORPORATION

business

AUTOMOBILES

design firm

RINEY, BRADFORD & HUBER

art director/ designer

HILLARY WOLF

photographer

JOHN HATCHER

The logo or masthead of this newsletter—uncharacteristic for a major corporation—is a delightful collection of metamorphic letters. The design is equally sprightly and underscores this auto company's goal to be one with its community of workers and users.

pages 8, frequency 3/year, quantity 909,000, software QuarkXPress

SHAW XPRESSION

client

SHAW INDUSTRIES

business

CARPET

design firm

WAGES DESIGN

art director

BOB WAGES

**designer/
illustrator**

LIONEL FERREIRA

photographers

ED THOMPSON
SHAW INDUSTRIES

This eight-page foldout for a carpet company slyly suggests the carpet itself. Each interlocking page is graced with a different, contemporary design. Continued on pages 142 through 145.

pages Roll Fold, quantity 3,000, software QuarkXPress, Adobe Illustrator, Adobe Photoshop

---

Shaw Xpression

in New Product

New Frontier Lives up to Its Name
For Corporate, Commercial, and Institutional Environments.

With this edition of Expressions we're pleased to introduce New Frontier. A small scale integrated pattern — colored, styled, and engineered for clients who want distinction and demand performance, but who may short-change you on time and budget. Imagine that!

For starters, New Frontier is as close to bullet-proof as carpet gets. An ultra-dense multitextured loop surface that will fend off the most punishing commercial traffic. ADA compliant for maximum roller mobility.

Supra Solution Q™ (solution dyed) fiber guarantees superb appearance-in-use, with built-in characteristics crucial for intensive use environments. Superior colorfastness. Natural resistance to spills, stains, and soiling. Ability to withstand aggressive cleaning and maintenance.

But best of all is the breadth of standard colorways. Corporate beiges and taupes. Tinted naturals for healthcare. Vivid saturated combinations for in-store and hospitality. Because each selection is composed of six self-shades and an accent, New Frontier interacts with just about anything — especially important in renovation.

New Frontier comes in three backing systems — enabling you to match performance, installation, and budget needs throughout a project. Broadloom from Shaw Commercial for general corporate applications. Carpet tile from Networx for open offices and underfloor accessibility. And Networx-72, a six-foot, high performance roll product, perfect for hospitals, schools, and airports.

Architect folders and memo samples will be available from your Shaw Commercial representative, or by calling **1-800-257-SHAW**. For information on custom derivatives, call Studio oneZone™ at **1-800-342-SHAW**.

For technical information, please ask for a copy of our publication entitled: **Supra Solution Q, Solution Dyed Nylon for Carpet of Lasting Durability**. Copyright 1993, Shaw Industries, Inc.

New Frontier from Shaw Commercial Carpets and Networx Modular Carpets.

---

in Application

The following article is summarized with permission, from the March 1994 special healthcare supplement to *Building Design & Construction* magazine, from the editors of Cahners Publishing.

Tsoi/Kobus Completes $6 Million Brigham and Women's Renovation.

Boston's renowned Brigham and Women's Hospital is an institution of grand scale, with two million square feet, spread over nine acres. Likened to washing the windows of a skyscraper, a project that starts again as soon as it finishes, B&W's remedial design requirements are a kaleidoscope of ongoing projects and sub-projects.

Coming to grips with the ever-evolving design needs of this mega facility is a job of daunting proportions. For that, Boston-based Tsoi/Kobus & Associates (interior architecture and design) looks back at a client relationship that began more than a decade ago. Dovetailing into a sustainable master plan, a major two-year renovation was recently completed. The budget was $6 million, including $229,000 in furniture alone.

Updated areas include: oncology care, in-patient surgery, and coronary intensive care — with accompanying patient rooms, waiting rooms, and administrative areas.

Tsoi/Kobus principal and spokesperson Rick Kobus, comments on the design criteria: "Though medical equipment varies, conceptual considerations remain consistent — recurrent soft soothing colors, specifically blues, greens, and neutral tones: avoidance of yellow, a color that aggravates the patient's pallor; utilization, where possible, of windows for maximum spread of daylight; amenities extending to families who often stay many hours; and bedroom furniture designed to offer functional and aesthetic rewards."

Importantly, Kobus stresses that no attempt was made to simulate a residential atmosphere. Instead, attention to patient sensitivities and appropriateness to function provided the overriding criteria.

We are pleased that Tsoi/Kobus and B&W selected Stratton Commercial Carpets from the Shaw Industries Commercial Business Group for ambulatory patient, outpatient, corridor, common, and administrative areas. Stratton products contain FlorSept™, a broad-spectrum antimicrobial which permanently protects carpet from microorganisms, inhibiting bacteria, mold, mildew, and odors in the healthcare facility.

Oncology reception.
Walls are cherry wood panel, provides protection against...

A
Publication of the
Shaw Industries Commercial Business Group

Summer, 1994

Shaw Xpression

The Women of Design Trunk Show features 33 steamer trunks, each developed by a prominent woman design professional.

in Partnership

California Winter Market Celebrates Women's Contribution to Design

Shaw Commercial and Steelcase Salute Beverly Russell

Beverly Russell's extensive journalism career has included editorial posts at Brides, House and Garden, and House Beautiful. Prior to embarking on her independent career in 1991, she served as Editor-in-Chief for Interior Design magazine for ten years. Among her many acclaimed books are House and Garden's Book of Remodeling, Designer's Workplaces, and Architecture and Design 1970 1990: New Ideas in America.

Ms. Russell's most recent book entitled Women of Design is a compendium of women's contribution to the field of contract interior design. Honoring this work, the Steelcase Design Partnership, an alliance of affiliated interior product companies, has sponsored a movable exhibition entitled The Women of Design Trunk Show.

The exhibition, which premiered at New York's Cooper Hewitt Museum, features seven foot steamer trunks designed by 33 prominent designers, reflecting the individual principles by which each woman addresses design challenges and arrives at unique solutions. The idea was conceived not only in celebration of Beverly Russell's book, but as an attraction for design, marketing and cultural events across America.

The California Winter Market — San Francisco Contemporary provided the perfect venue for the exhibition. In recognition, Ms. Russell chaired two plenary sessions sponsored by Shaw Commercial Carpets. On January 24 — a symposium honoring Bay Area women participating in the Trunk Show; Phyllis Martin-Vegue (Martin Vegue Winkelstein & Morris), Carolyn Iu (Skidmore Owings & Merrill), Pam Babey (Babey Moulton), and Luna Howard (Ace Architects); and on January 25 — an illustrated lecture bringing to life the many achievements portrayed in her book, followed by a closing reception/dinner at the upscale Sheraton Palace Hotel.

Billed jointly, The California Winter Market is an annual event for the residential and retail design trade; the San Francisco Contemporary features permanent showrooms with interior products from more than 2500 manufacturers.

The Shaw Industries Commercial Business Group is pleased to salute the achievements women have made to shape today's contract interior industry. For further information on the The Women of Design Trunk Show, contact Tammy Fulcher-Muraski at the Steelcase Design Partnership, 616-698-1608.

---

in Context

Schedule for Business Opportunity Workshops Firmed Up

Responding to accolades for last year's tour, the Shaw Industries Commercial Business Group has firmed-up the 1994 schedule for its business opportunity workshops. Developed for design professionals, the curriculum focuses on obtaining and maintaining new business — from the design firm's perspective. Specific topics of discussion will include: securing appointments with top executives; differentiating your firm; handling stalls and pricing resistance; turning objections into winning projects; and marketing your design firm.

The day long seminars, each limited to 30 attendees, will include a continental breakfast and luncheon, plus a reception afterwards, allowing participants to renew acquaintances and establish contacts. Participants will receive .70 CEU credits.

Along with Shaw Commercial, cosponsors include Interiors magazine, DuPont Flooring Systems, and Steelcase. For reservations, please contact John Rouse at Interiors magazine. Tel: 312 464 8515. Fax: 312 464 8510.

SEATTLE	JUNE 27
PORTLAND	JUNE 28
SAN FRANCISCO	JUNE 29 & 30
CLEVELAND	AUG. 8
CINCINNATI	AUG. 9
PITTSBURGH	AUG. 10
KANSAS CITY	AUG. 11
ST. LOUIS	AUG. 12
NEW YORK	SEPT 12 & OCT. 5
BOSTON	SEPT 13
PHILADELPHIA	SEPT 14
DENVER	SEPT 20
SALT LAKE CITY	SEPT 21
DETROIT	SEPT 22
INDIANAPOLIS	SEPT 23
TORONTO	OCT. 3
WASHINGTON	OCT. 4
ATLANTA	OCT. 17
DALLAS	OCT 18 & 19
HOUSTON	OCT 20
PHOENIX	OCT 25
LOS ANGELES	OCT 26 & 27

Shaw / Paul Singer Premier Joint Venue at Westweek '94

$2,500 Pledged to IBD Scholarship Fund

In 1989, the IBD Southern California Chapter created the Calibre Awards to recognize those companies who exemplify commitment and support of quality design. Six years later, it is still Southern California's prestige industry awards ceremony. It enjoys the status of being the opening event for Westweek, the West Coast's largest annual market event.

Those attending the Calibre Awards Dinner during Westweek '94 learned about the joint effort of Paul Singer Floor Coverings and the Shaw Industries Commercial Business Group to benefit the IBD Scholarship Fund, pledging five dollars in the name of the first 500 guests to visit the Paul Singer showroom in the Pacific Design Center — for a total of $2,500.

Westweek '94 was especially significant, in that it marked the premier market showing of the newly organized Shaw Industries Commercial Business Group, featuring the combined capabilities of Shaw Commercial Carpets, Stratton Commercial Carpets, Network Modular Carpets, and Shaw Rugs. For design professionals, this resource now offers the world's most comprehensive and interactive selection of commercial carpet products.

september | october

1 2 3 4 5 6 7 8 9 10 11 12 13 14 15 16 17 18 19 20 21 22 23 24 25 26 27 28 29 30   1 2 3 4 5 6 7 8 9 10 11 12 13 14 15 16 17 18 19 20 21

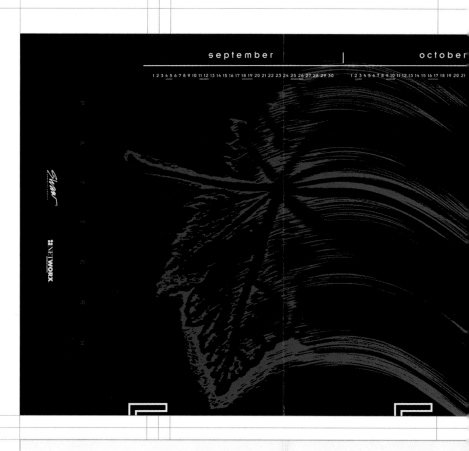

expressions

in New Products

Wildcreek & Millennium — The Newest Systems Introduction

In this issue of *Expressions*, we're pleased to enclose a sample of our newest systems introduction, a multi-textured organic pattern available in 17 standard colorways: *Wildcreek* from Shaw Commercial® Carpets and *Millennium* from Networx® Modular Carpets. Custom derivatives are available exclusively through *Studio One 2 One™* (please see adjoining article). Construction is a dense tenth gauge pile for exceptional long-term appearance.

Wildcreek & Millennium are offered in three separate backing technologies — a systems approach that enables you to more precisely match performance, installation, and budget requirements throughout a project, while utilizing a consistent finish.

Wildcreek / Broadloom from Shaw Commercial Carpets is for general commercial applications. It can be installed conventionally; or with Shaw's *Advantage System™* dry bond membrane — our environmentally-friendly product which eliminates the odors, curing time, and fumes of wet adhesives. And for a modest minimum, Wildcreek broadloom is also available with Enhancer® high-performance attached cushion backing.

Millennium / Networx-72 from Networx is our six-foot, high-performance roll product, engineered for intensive-use areas such as hospitals, schools, and airports. Its thermoplastic moisture-proof backing won't stretch, absorb spills, or buckle under traffic. And its bonded seams are guaranteed never to split or separate.

Wildcreek
& Millennium:
Three backing
technologies
help match
performance,
installation,
and budget
requirements.

Millennium / Carpet Tile from Networx is the preferred medium for open offices and areas requiring constant change and underfloor accessibility. Networx carpet tiles can be installed glue-free for ultimate flexibility.

Wildcreek & Millennium are produced with DuPont Antron Legacy® advanced generation nylon for maximum maintainability. They are also protected by DuPont DuraTech® soil protector, have permanent built-in anti-static properties, and demonstrate excellent colorfastness to light and atmospheric contaminants.

Wildcreek & Millennium products carry extended performance warranties for a wide range of end-use conditions. Architect folders and memo samples are now available from your Shaw Commercial or Networx representative — or by calling 1-800-257-7429.

in Installations

Environmental Responsibility in Washington State

Note: The following is summarized with permission from the May 1993 issue of *Facilities Design & Management*. Photography by Nick Merrick, Hedrich Blessing.

Jack Brown, former assistant director for Washington's Department of General Administration, wanted more than just another facility when he accepted responsibility for overseeing the construction of the state's new *Department of Natural Resources Building*. Brown learned from past experience that indoor air quality (IAQ) was an interactive function of building design, interior product selection, and long-term maintenance.

In his quest for a qu[...]
the IAQ specialty firm[...]
Atlanta. AQS's missio[...]
criteria in which ten[...]
specifications includ[...]
control at the source [...]
building (use and mai[...]

Every prospective int[...]
with stringent off-gas[...]
including particulat[...]
organic compounds (V[...]

expressions

in Context

Catalyst, fusion bonded carpet tile from Networx, is used in open office plans. Interiors and architecture by C.W. Fentress J.H. Bradburn & Associates.

Interior product specifications were developed by the firm of C.W. Fentress J.H. Bradburn & Associates of Denver. Floor covering products included both carpet tile and broadloom products which had to conform to strict IAQ standards set by AQS.

In a rigorous preliminary testing program, products from both Shaw Commercial Carpets and Networx Modular Carpets were submitted and approved. By competitive bid, Catalyst, a fusion bonded carpet tile product from Networx, along with a coordinating broadloom product from Shaw Commercial, was chosen.

The commercial divisions of Shaw Industries are pleased to be contributing partners in the success of Jack Brown's vision.

Note: At press time, a second IAQ-sensitive project in Washington's Department of Ecology is being installed. We are pleased that another carpet tile product from Networx was selected.

Architect Curt Fentress designed the building to be compatible with others within the Washington State Capitol Campus at Olympia.

Shaw Hosts 12-City CEU Tour

Shaw Commercial Carpets recently co-sponsored a series of CEU workshops for designers and architects, conducted in twelve U.S. cities. The curriculum centered around obtaining and developing new business — from the professional design firm's perspective. Other sponsors included Interiors magazine, DuPont Flooring Systems, and Steelcase.

The seminars covered a variety of topics, including:

- Arranging appointments with top executives.
- Differentiating your firm.
- Handling stalls, delays, and pricing resistance.
- Turning objections into winning situations.
- Developing reasons to do business with your firm.

A reception capped off each day-long seminar, allowing participants to renew acquaintances and establish contacts. Many thanks to our generous co-sponsors — and especially the participants around the country for making this series a delightful experience. We've had scores of requests to do it again!

Shaw Commercial and Networx Debut Design Studio

Shaw Commercial and Networx officially opened their new Design Studio in Cartersville, Georgia this past July. Located an hour north of Atlanta's Hartsfield International Airport, just off I-75, it is the industry's most comprehensive commercial carpet development facility equipped to assist interior designers, facility planners, and architects. A part of the Design Studio is Studio One 2 One, our personalized service center which opens up the same development capabilities by telephone.

The heartbeat of the Design Studio is the world's most complete pilot plant for commercial carpet products, with virtually every manufacturing technique duplicated, machine by machine.

For planning decisions and complex projects, clients are invited to use Design Flex™, Shaw's proprietary CAD system developed exclusively for carpet. Simple exercises like reversing a colorway or changing yarn placement can be performed routinely from on-hand components, while complex development — starting from scratch — can be accomplished in a matter of days.

To assist in the development process, we also maintain an extensive library of resource materials — decorative fabrics, laminates, ceramics, stones — allowing you to coordinate your products with other current finishes and surfaces.

By visiting the Design Studio, or by calling Studio One 2 One, you will work directly with design professionals who will help evaluate many alternatives, based on our own experience — including technical information, as well as recommendations on the use of custom color and pattern.

Every request, large or small, simple or complicated, carries with it our dedication to design integrity.

If you would like more information about visiting the Design Studio or about Studio One 2 One services, call 1-800-342-7429.

Carpet and Indoor Air Quality

Last October 29, CBS-TV aired an edition of Street Stories, hosted by Ed Bradley of 60-Minutes. It focused on a group of people who allege health problems associated with their carpet. Supporting their claims was Dr. Rosalind Anderson of Anderson Laboratories, a Massachusetts for-profit testing lab. By any account, the tabloid report was edited for emotional impact and slanted so cast doubts on the safety of carpet. It was pretty unfair.

The U.S. carpet industry spans five decades, with billions of square yards installed. Since the components of carpet have changed very little, there is considerable confidence in the safety of our raw materials. Adverse health effects have usually been isolated and almost always have been the result of some other local factor.

Unfortunately, carpet has been associated with a group of highly publicized interior contaminants called volatile organic compounds — known as VOC's. VOC's are an inherent by-product of both man-made and natural products: woods, plastics, fibers, varnishes, coatings, and cleaning chemicals — to name but a few. VOC's are invisible, and frequently odorless. Unfortunately, the media has distorted the issue by attacking the sources of VOC's, product by product, without a clear point of reference.

VOC's from a wide variety of products used to build, furnish, and maintain our commercial interiors do have the potential to impact indoor air quality when confined in a closed building. However, as a practical matter, the issue is not their total elimination. We now understand that the real issue is proper management of VOC's by good building design, product selection, and maintenance methods.

Also, please be aware of the confusion between carpet odor and actual toxicity. 4-Phenylcyclohexene (commonly known as 4PC), an ingredient of latex carpet backing, is the source of the familiar new carpet odor, a common VOC that dissipates rapidly after installation with carpet ventilation. Independent testing at 4PC, even in exaggerated concentrations, shows its actual toxicity, if any, to be almost unmeasurable. Even so, because some have found it objectionable, Shaw Industries is actively working to minimize this characteristic.

Carpet has taken considerable flack about VOC's. Therefore, in the absence of Federal standards, the CRI (Carpet and Rug Institute) has launched an ambitious testing program. Although there are various carpet categories, maximum base line emissions have been established at 0.6 micrograms per square meter, per hour. By contrast, other common interior products — paints, coatings, varnishes, and even certain wood products — demonstrate many times those emissions.

Currently, close to 90% of all carpet products made in the U.S. have been accepted into the CRI testing program. Shaw Industries actively endorses the efforts of this program. For more detailed information, please contact the Carpet and Rug Institute, P.O. Box 2048, Dalton, GA 30722. Telephone 706-278-3176.

Private offices, such as the Commissioner's office, are a small percentage of total workspace in Washington's Department of Natural Resources Building.

Shaw Commercial Carpets / Networx Modular Carpets

by Shaw Industries, Inc., P.O.Drawer 2128, Dalton, GA 30722-2128, 800-441-SHAW

GCC/NW1281193AX

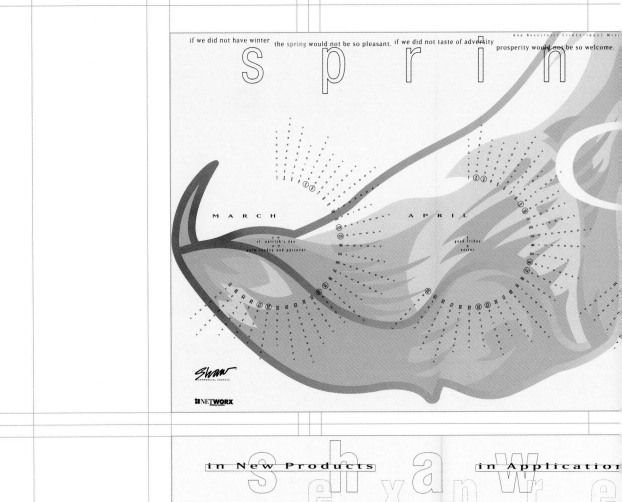

in New Products

Updated Classic for Corporate Clients — Shaw Commercial Adds *Palace Guard* to the *Regal Collection*

Contemporary Classic — In response to the requirements of design professionals, Shaw Commercial's *Regal Collection*, offers a comprehensive range of commercial carpet products, inspired by the elements of classic design. With this edition of *Expressions*, we are pleased to introduce the newest addition to the *Regal Collection* — *Palace Guard*.

Corporate Plus More — Inspired by a back-to-basics styling, *Palace Guard* is a classic small scale graphic multitexture, featuring a rich dominant tip sheared field with subtle, yet distinctive loop counterpoints. An ample twenty-one standard colorways have been developed for the corporate client. However, the traditional business palette has been supplemented with a range of more eclectic combinations — making it appropriate for public space and hospitality applications.

Performance Assurance — In keeping with Shaw Commercial's commitment to meeting complex long term appearance-in-use expectations, *Palace Guard* is crafted in a dense tenth gauge face fabric from advanced generation DuPont Legacy continuous filament nylon. Yarn dyed colorations enable crisp, saturated combinations. *Palace Guard* is covered by Shaw Commercial's comprehensive 10-year limited performance warranty.

Try Your Own Hand — As always, the standard colorations of *Palace Guard* will be available for immediate service from in-depth inventory. Alternatively, Shaw Commercial welcomes custom development requests through its on-staff team of design professionals at *Studio one2one™*.

Technical and Design Support — Much more than design solutions, *Studio one2one* is also set up to assist with technical recommendations on proper engineering, to offer practical advice on color and performance, and to help coordinate Shaw Commercial products with other interior systems and surfaces. *Studio one2one* — **1-800-342-SHAW**.

Samples Soon Available — Architect folders and memo samples will soon be available on *Palace Guard* from your Shaw Commercial representative, or by calling the commercial sample response team at **1-800-257-SHAW**.

Palace Guard from Shaw Commercial's Regal Collection
Twenty-one standard colorways feature rich multitextured fields with subtle counterpoints. Shown here, and also enclosed with this edition of **Expressions**, standard colorway 17324 Olivet.

in Applicatio[n]

The following article is summarized, with permission, from the November 1993 issue of *Interior Design*.

IBD 1993 Outstanding Achievement Award Winner
— NASA Auditorium, Washington, DC.

When The National Aeronautical Space Administration (NASA) commissioned the Washington interior architecture and design firm of Greenwell Goetz to update the 4,000 square foot, 236-seat auditorium at its national headquarters, the client set a simple overarching objective — *to evoke a sense of NASA and its spirit for exploration and mission.*

Architectural restrictions in the multipurpose space included an extremely low slab-to-ceiling height and a fixed stage location. Major design criteria included ADA (Americans with Disabilities Act) compliance, along with complex acoustica[l] and audio-visual requirements.

According to Lewis J. Goetz, *principal in charge*, the design team approached the design in a way similar to NASA's own uniq[ue] economical attitude toward space exploratio[n ...] *ment of interconnected disassembled p[...]*

The central design element is a wave-sh[...] developed to absorb and reflect sound[...] support both architectural and theatrica[l ...] in part, by installing towers on either [...]

Major interior materials included alumin[um ...] channels, wood, and graphite-colored [...] surfaces. We are especially pleased th[at ...] Commercial Carpet as the predominant floorin[g ...]

Added Goetz: *We took a nuts and bolts, utilitarian[...] and a reason.* The project was awarded a covete[d ...] last year's Midnight Affair in conjunction with Chic[...]

Behind-the-scene view of
side corridor and stairs,
exemplifying the simplicity
and integrity of the alu-
minum and stainless steel
surface materials.

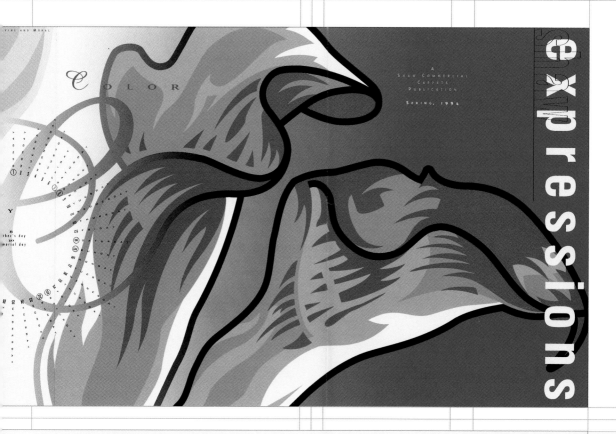

expressions

C O L O R

A
SHAW COMMERCIAL
CARPETS
PUBLICATION

SPRING, 1994

Shaw Publishes *Carpet and the Interior Environment*

The *Shaw Industries Commercial Business Group* has recently released a publication entitled *Carpet and the Interior Environment*. Posed in a succinct question and answer format, the graphically attractive pamphlet was sent directly to some 35,000 design and facility professionals, including the active membership of IBD, ASID, IFMA, and BOMA.

The purpose of the writing is to report on the status of current research relative to the impact of carpet on the indoor air quality of the workplace. The result is a balanced approach to understanding and evaluating IAQ issues — with respect to all interior products — based on good science, as contrasted with unsupported assumptions which are frequently disseminated by the media. The publication has been applauded by both industry and design leaders as being both educational and highly informative.

Additional copies are available from your local Shaw representative, or by faxing your request to the Commercial Business Group at 706-275-3358.

Shaw Industries Commercial Business Group Sponsors IBD National Board Meeting in Atlanta

Shaw Industries Commercial Business Group — which is composed of Shaw Commercial Carpets, Stratton Commercial Carpets, Network Modular Carpets, and Hospitality Designs — is pleased to have co-sponsored the annual IBD National Board of Directors Meeting in Atlanta on February 7.

In cooperation with IBD's continuing education program, Shaw conducted a special focus group with ten design firm principals in attendance. The four-hour session was divided into timely areas of concern — each an area in which Shaw Industries has taken a proactive approach: environmental issues, indoor air quality, carpet performance, custom carpet development, and carpet styling trends.

Shaw Industries is a member of the IBD Industry Foundation.

Shaw Thomson Plant Receives ISO-9000 Registration

Quality-oriented issues have become part and parcel to both manufacturing and specifying interior products. In concert with those objectives, *Shaw Industries* recently announced that its Thomson Extrusion Facility located in Thomson, Georgia, is the first carpet manufacturing plant in the United States to achieve certification by the British Standards Institution for compliance with ISO-9000 Series registration. The plant manufactures continuous filament extruded carpet fiber.

By defining exactly what customer requirements are, and how those needs are met, the ISO-9000 Series registration provides important benefits for customers of certified companies. Third-party certification indicates appropriate quality systems for specific products and services.

Many manufacturing facilities have required 18 to 36 months for compliance. The Thomson facility, however, was able to meet all standards within six months.

Shaw Commercial to Host Business Opportunity Workshops

In response to a successful 1993 tour, Shaw Commercial Carpets has announced it will again co-sponsor a series of business opportunity workshops for designers and architects, to be held in several U.S. cities. The full schedule is yet to be announced. The curriculum will center around obtaining and developing new business — from the professional design firm's perspective. Specific topics of discussion will include:

• Securing appointments with top executives.

• Differentiating your firm.

• Handling stalls and pricing resistance.

• Turning objections into winning projects.

• Marketing your design firm.

Each day-long seminar will include a continental breakfast and luncheon, plus a reception afterwards, allowing participants to renew acquaintances and establish contacts. Participants will receive .70 CEU credits.

Along with *Shaw Commercial*, co-sponsors include *Interiors* magazine, *DuPont Flooring Systems*, and *Steelcase*. For schedules and reservations, please contact Quetzy Vasquez at *Interiors* magazine, Tel: 212-536-5141, Fax: 212-536-5357, or contact your Shaw Commercial or Networx Modular representative for further details.

in Context

Concrete from Carpet. Shaw's New R&D Building Promises Even More.

Back in 1989, when Shaw Industries founder Robert E. Shaw first began issuing internal environmental mandates, his goal was to lay the foundation for an *Environmental Friendly Culture*. Little did he know it would literally lay the foundation for Shaw's new R&D Building — and change the way engineers the world over think about reinforced concrete as a building material.

It all started with a short-range goal — no process materials from Shaw's manufacturing operations would be landfilled by 1996 — which quickly evolved into a long-range goal — to develop proactive programs to keep disposed carpet out of the world's landfills. Who better to tackle this than the world's largest manufacturer and marketer of carpet products?

Jack C. Buchanan
Corporate Recycling Coordinator
for Shaw Industries

The cast of characters in this undertaking coalesced within only a few months. Little more than a year ago, Jack C. Buchanan, *Corporate Recycling Coordinator* for Shaw Industries, also a member of Shaw's R&TD (Research and Technology Development) team, heard about Dr. Youjiang Wang of Georgia Tech's School of Textiles and Fibers.

Dr. Youjiang Wang

It seems Dr. Wang had recently presented extraordinary findings to a research group dedicated to recovery and reuse of materials in highway construction. By coincidence, Buchanan had spearheaded concurrent studies — independent of Dr. Wang's efforts — to process carpet waste into construction materials.

Shaw Industries' new R&D Center, now under construction, located on the south side of the company's Dalton, Georgia corporate campus. Architecture and Design: Bull, Brown, and Kilgo Architects, AIA, Atlanta.

Thus, the catalyst for joining forces was swift and logical. And what better timing than the opportunity for a real-world laboratory testing — Shaw's new *Research and Development Center*, just off the drawing board. Buchanan quickly enlisted the support of Don Brumbelow, *Shaw Facilities Manager*, and head of corporate construction whose contacts and expertise in the construction trade provided the final invaluable link between idea and reality.

The premise is eloquently simple: replace a portion of conventional concrete substrate with shredded carpet scraps. Laboratory tests have resulted in a hybrid composite product with remarkable properties, equal to, and in many ways superior to, conventional concrete.

The floors, sidewalks, driveways, and curbs of the R&D Center will be constructed of the new admixture. Pouring is being monitored by a research team headed by Dr. Wang, including structural and testing engineers. Work is being documented by video tape and will be used to publish a thesis for peer review.

The goal of the project is to assist Georgia Tech in securing additional funding to continue research in recycling carpet into building material. If predictions hold true, it is entirely possible that the demand for discarded carpet products as a result of this research could ultimately outstrip the supply available — effectively fulfilling Mr. Shaw's mandate to keep carpet out of the world's landfills.

Shaw Commercial Carpets / Networx Modular Carpets by Shaw Industries, Inc., P. O. Drawer 2128, Dalton, GA 30722-2128, 1-800-241-SHAW
StudioˈoneZone™ is an official trademark of Shaw Industries, Inc.; registration applied for and pending. All rights reserved.
SCC/NW 12803594XX Printed in U.S.A.

PORTFOLIO
DEALS OF THE YEAR

I nvestment bankers usually do their work far from the limelight, helping clients raise capital in the public and private markets or execute a merger, acquisition or divestiture. But once a year, *Institutional Investor* magazine turns the spotlight on the firms that make these transactions happen in its annual "Deals of the Year" feature. ✍$ This year, 10 transactions in which Lehman Brothers played a role were selected as among the most noteworthy domestic and international deals of 1992, the highest number ever for the firm. Following is a look at each of these transactions. *See page four*

PORTFOLIO

client

SHEARSON LEHMAN BROTHERS

business

INVESTMENTS

design firm

THE BARNETT GROUP, INC.

art directors

DAVID BARNETT THEO FELS

designers

THEO FELS
(top)

DAVID BARNETT
(bottom, right)

illustrators

PAUL RIVOCHE JEFF KOEGEL

One-half fold is a full illustration, the other half is a table of contents with referral lines. When opened, a full-page conceptual illustration acts as a poster that announces the theme of each issue.

pages 8, frequency Monthly, quantity 40,000, software QuarkXPress

PORTFOLIO

RIGHT ON TRAK

> SLB's billion-dollar baby comes of age <

EXCHANGE

client

LEARNING INTERNATIONAL

business

TRAINING PROGRAMS

design firm

BERNHARDT FUDYMA DESIGN GROUP

illustrator

DAVE CUTLER

This long and narrow newsletter is folded in half to make a square. The top portion is a conceptual illustration, while under the fold is a handsomely illustrated table of contents.

pages 8-12, frequency Quarterly, quantity 7,500

COMMUNIQUÉ

client

ERNST & YOUNG

business

ACCOUNTING

design firm

THE BARNETT GROUP

art directors

DAVID BARNETT DRALYN VEECH

designers

KATHY WOODS DRALYN VEECH

illustrators

DAVID SHANNON LINDA BLECK

This two-color newsletter avoids black, even in the conceptual illustration that runs throughout.

pages 8, frequency Quarterly, quantity 20,000, software QuarkXPress

A league of our own

Early last month, the much-rumored entry of General Motors and General Electric into the consumer credit card industry finally took place—and with considerably less fanfare than accompanied AT&T Universal Card Services' launch in 1990.

GE launched a few days ahead of GM—presumably in an effort to steal GM's thunder. GE's card carries an 18.4 annual percentage rate (APR) and an annual fee. "It's not in tune with the market at all," said Robert McKinly, president of RAM Research.

The press was focused on the automotive giant's impending announcement and gave GE little coverage.

GM garnered more publicity but virtually every story positioned both GM and GE as following UCS' lead. *Investor's Business Daily*, for example, said, "Both companies are trying to match the success of American Telephone & Telegraph Co.'s Universal Card. ...It's unclear whether

GM can match the spectacular success AT&T achieved."

Both GM and GE offer rebate programs (see page 7 for details). "My feeling is they're more of a threat to other issuers, such as Discover," said Keith Kendrick, senior vice president Marketing Development.

GM's and GE's entries are a challenge, not a threat, Kendrick added, and Bill Farris, senior vice president Universal Card Product Management, agrees. "We have a very high value product," he says.

Our APR is one of the lowest in the business, Farris notes, and is variable, tied to the prime rate (the rate banks charge their best customers); UCS recently lowered its

APR for the fifth time to 14.9 percent. "And it's available to all our customers, not just a select few the way Citibank operates. UCS is also the only significant issuer with a free-for-life card."

UCS customers like the assurance of the AT&T name and the general acceptance of the card, Kendrick adds. "UCS offers quality, value, and unparalleled service—a triple threat—and in service we're in a league of our own.

"We have a tendency to underrate ourselves," he goes on. "We aren't just another utility infielder. UCS, by any standard, qualifies for the Most Valuable Player award—and our customers know it."

by Laura M. Haywood

UNIVERSE

client

AT&T

business

CREDIT/CALLING CARD

design firm

HUSK JENNINGS ADVERTISING

art director/designer

MIKE BOYLES

illustrator

RUSS WILSON

Each cover has a huge logo emblazoned over an always changing illustration. While the cover is altered, the inside layouts are rather consistent. Changes in scale create visual impact.

pages 8-12, frequency Monthly, quantity 3,000, software QuarkXPress

---

A Newsletter from American Express

Winter 1991–92

Inside

2 Handling the Holidays

We Want to Hear from You

3 Vacationing with Three Generations

4 Great Trips at Great Prices

Splurging on Gifts is Easy

5 Senior Membership Values

7 Extending the Family

8 Shopping Insurance

Retirement and Estate Planning

SENIOR MEMBERSHIP

REWARDS

CAREERS: THE SECOND TIME AROUND

From building a business to transferring job skills, you might find a second career even more fulfilling than your first.

For many, the step off the top of the ladder in one career can be a step onto an exciting first rung in another. More and more retirees feel it's never too late to start a second career. Increasingly, employers too "are recognizing the value of veteran professionals," says Shirley R. Brussell, executive director of Operation ABLE, a Chicago-based nonprofit agency that helps create employment opportunities for those over 45 and over.

According to Brussell, older employees bring a wealth of experience to a job—not only their skills, but qualities like patience and commitment. Also, they can serve as positive role models for younger employees when working closely with them.

Those wishing to establish themselves in a less traditional, or more personal, career, might consider pinpointing a passion and then putting it to work, advises Lydia Brontë, Ph.D., author of *The Longevity Factor: How the New Reality of Extended Careers is Leading to Richer Lives* (to be published in

August 1992 by HarperCollins). Brontë urges seniors to focus on something they genuinely enjoy doing.

You can discover what that might be by compiling a list of the accomplishments you're most proud of and then noting what they have in common.

Once you've narrowed down your interests, consider seeking out other people in those lines of work. By talking to them, you'll gain a better feel for how to proceed.

One excellent way to gain experience and broaden your network: Volunteer at a firm in your prospective career field. Or consider signing up with a temporary-employment agency that places workers in the field in which you're interested. And keep your ears open: Even if the company you break into doesn't have a paid or full-time position available, you might hear of a job you would like at a similar company.

If you want to go into business for yourself, consult others who have started a comparable business—but not in your geographical area. "They'll be more willing to help you if they know you won't be competing with them," says Brontë.

To decide what type of business you might like to run, focus on your talents—such as technical know-how and customer relations—and your past work experience. According to a spokesman at the U.S. Small

Continued on page 7

1 REWARDS

REWARDS

client

AMERICAN EXPRESS

business

CREDIT CARD

design firm

STUDIO MORRIS

art director/designer

JEFF MORRIS

For a conservative company, this conservative, but nevertheless contemporary, looking newsletter is appropriate. The use of full color gives this the look of a typical travel or food magazine.

pages 8, frequency Quarterly, quantity 5,000, software QuarkXPress, Adobe Photoshop

THE INDIVIDUAL BANKER

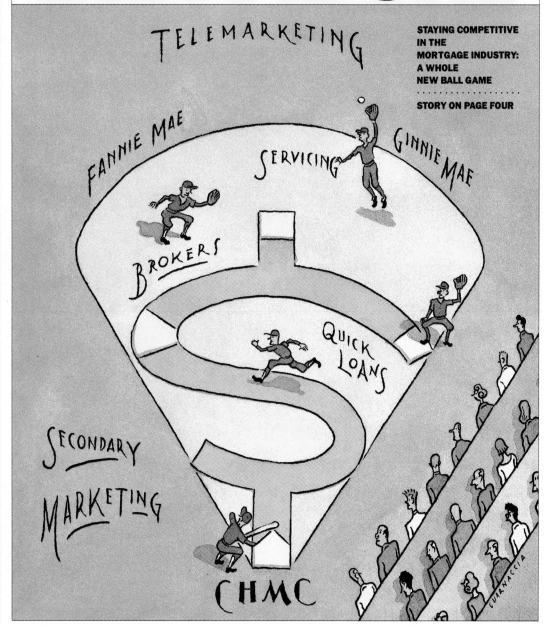

STAYING COMPETITIVE
IN THE
MORTGAGE INDUSTRY:
A WHOLE
NEW BALL GAME

STORY ON PAGE FOUR

A Whole New BALLGAME

For Zsa Zsa Gabor, it's husbands; for George Steinbrenner, managers; for Kellogg's, raisins in the bran ...the stuff of life that each can never have enough of. For Chase Home Mortgage Corporation (CHMC), it's quality mortgages. The more it can originate, service, buy and sell, the better.

But the question nowadays is how best to go about it. Attractive interest rates have drawn more home buyers to market, and mortgages are hot properties—not only for consumers, but also for investors attracted by high yields on the loans.

To profitably pursue its obsession, CHMC must adapt to a more competitive, expanding industry by growing along with it—upgrading systems, finding new ways to reach customers and deal in the secondary market, building its servicing portfolio and opening offices.

Increasing its office network to 29, CHMC has already opened branches this year in Orange, California; Ft. Lauderdale, Florida; and—in conjunction with Chase Bank of Florida—Sarasota.

"By year end," says Jim Panepinto, National Production executive, "we will have added three offices in California and one in Virginia."

In addition, CHMC's purchase of Freedom Mortgage Company of Tampa, Florida, opens two new markets: Atlanta, Georgia, and Ft. Myers, Florida.

"Through offices, we can originate mortgages directly with our customers," says Mr. Panepinto, "in addition to our traditional approach of working through realtors, brokers and developers."

The Montvale, New Jersey-based subsidiary is tampering with this same tradition in the tri-state area of New York, New Jersey and Connecticut. But not by adding offices.

"We're advertising," says Mr. Panepinto, brandishing a copy of *New York Newsday.* Interested readers call a toll-free number to reach a new telemarketing center in Montvale.

"This will help lower our cost of acquiring business," says Mr. Panepinto. "Very strong initial response indicates that our customers are as positive as we are about the service."

A direct mail campaign to local Chase customers is expected soon, and telemarketing centers are being considered for other regions.

To handle an increase in originations, the company is automating its manual processing. The system—to be installed in all offices—is a kind of mortgage monitor that will keep tabs on loans from the time applications are received until closings. The system can also be installed in regional bank branches and realtor offices, linking them directly with CHMC. It is one example of how CHMC is using technology to expand its presence.

If projections are correct, CHMC will appreciate the help the system offers. The company, which topped $1 billion in originations last year, plans to better that in 1987.

And with more mortgages coming in, CHMC is faced with what to do with them. Changes in the secondary market, where CHMC sells mortgages, have increased the options.

Many of CHMC's products do not conform to specifications required by government mortgage agencies, which traditionally bought the bulk of its loans.

"Not that others aren't interested," says Sam Cooper, Product Management executive. He notes that new buyers, like the big investment houses of First Boston and Goldman Sachs, ensure that "virtually anything can be sold." And in many shapes and sizes.

"Loans used to be offered whole," he explains. "Now they're broken up to bring the best price." For example, CHMC can sell a mortgage's interest to a buyer looking for rising rates, and its principal to another one looking for a drop.

This sophisticated market has demanded a more active approach toward monitoring portfolios. "We sell some loans immediately," says Mr. Cooper, "but a growing number are being held until they've built a good credit rating and the timing is right for sale."

Finding the right moment is just as important when it comes to buying.

At his desk by 7:30 a.m., Mr. Cooper spends his day dealing on the phone. "I find out what's offered and what my deadline is for deciding." Quick discussions with staff follow, as prices, risks and other essentials are weighed.

CHMC plans to buy up to $500 million in mortgages this year, in conjunction with Chase's regional banks—eager to build assets—in Florida, Maryland and Ohio.

"The regional banks will hold the mortgages in their portfolios," explains Mr. Cooper, "and we'll do the servicing, handling payments and the like."

The arrangement fits in fine with CHMC's 1987 plans to increase its servicing portfolio by 57 percent, from its $3.5 billion base.

Says Bill Frontera, National Servicing executive, "A big boost will also come from buying the servicing operations of other companies." Like the $1 billion portfolio CHMC has acquired from Freedom Mortgage. That acquisition alone is boosting CHMC's portfolio by 29 percent, as well as providing an additional servicing plant.

These new acquisitions are feeding not only CHMC's magnificent obsession with pursuing mortgages but also its bottom line. Leave the "less is more" philosophy to interior designers. For CHMC, "more" means money.

—*Philip E. Natoli*

Chase Home Mortgage is playing tough in a major-league business, with a balanced lineup of services.

CHASE HOME MORTGAGE CORPORATION

THE INDIVIDUAL BANKER

client

CHASE MANHATTAN

business

BANKING

design firm

TANA & CO.

art director

KEITH MCDAVID

designer

TANA KAMINE

illustrator

STEVEN GUARNACCIA

This four-color newsletter is a tour de force if only for the repertory of major illustrators used throughout. In addition, the expressive typography is a joy to the eye.

pages 8, frequency Bimonthly, typography Photographic Typesetting

LEEWARDEN INFORMATIEF

client

CITY OF LEEWARDEN

business

LOCAL AUTHORITIES

design firm

TOTAL DESIGN

art director

WIM WESTERVELD

designer

SUSAN SELLERS

This oddly folded newsletter—not just in halves or quarters but in curious partials—unfolds into a large broadsheet with information on one side and a poster image on the verso.

pages foldout, *frequency* Monthly, *quantity* 10,000, *software* QuarkXPress

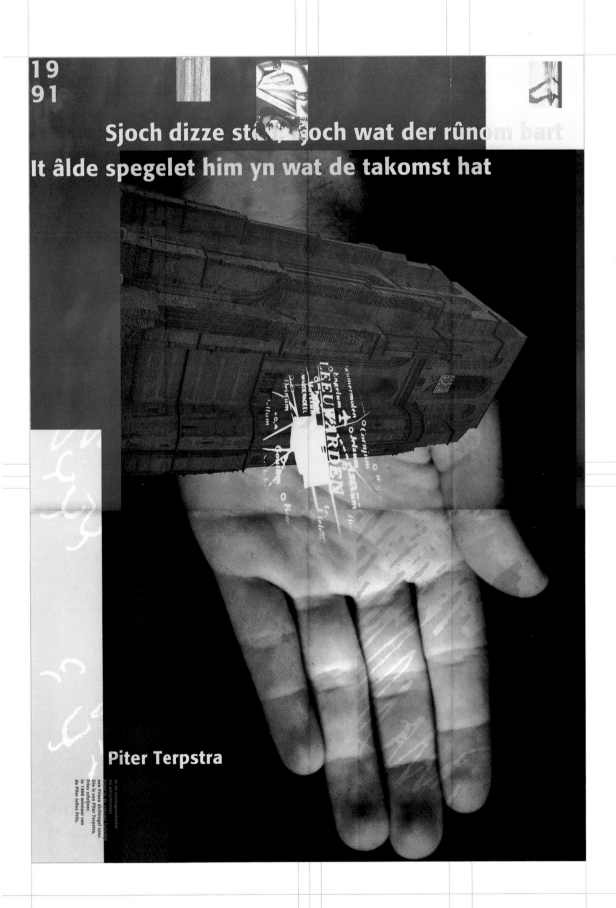

Sjoch dizze st... ...och wat der rûnom bart

It âlde spegelet him yn wat de takomst hat

Piter Terpstra

In de correspondentie
en advertinsjes fan dit blêdsji
komt de namme foar fan
een Fries dichtregel foar.
Die is fan Piter Terpstra,
Fries schrijver,
in 1988 winnaar van
de Piter Jelles Priis.

Design Firms

Alexander Isley Design
580 Broadway, Suite 715
New York, New York 10012
Tel: (212) 941-7945

Allemann/Almquist + Jones
301 Cherry Street, Third Floor
Philadelphia, Pennsylvania 19106
Tel: (215) 829-9442
Fax: (215) 829-1755

Art Center College of Design
1700 Lida Street
Pasadena, California 91103
Tel: (818) 396-2384
Fax: (818) 729-1592

The **B**arnett Group
270 Lafayette Street
New York, New York 10012
Tel: (212) 431-7130
Fax: (212) 219-8976

BCM Graphics
1145 Brooklyn Avenue
Brooklyn, New York 11213
Tel: (718) 735-4444
Fax: (718) 604-7442

Bernhardt Fudyma Design Group
133 East 36th Street
New York, New York 10016
Tel: (212) 889-9337
Fax: (212) 889-8007

Greg Bonnell-Kangas
The Ohio State University
1125 Kinnear Road
Columbus, Ohio 43212
Tel: (614) 292-8214
Fax: (614) 292-0154

Brainstorm, Inc.
3347 Halifax
Dallas, Texas 75247
Tel: (214) 951-7791
Fax: (214) 951-9060

Calfo/Aron, Inc.
156 Fifth Avenue
New York, New York 10010
Tel: (212) 627-3802

Coleman Souter Design
639 Front Street
San Francisco, California 94111
Tel: (415) 543-7966
Fax: (415) 243-8157

Columbus College of Art and Design
107 North 9th Street
Columbus, Ohio 43215
Tel: (614) 224-09101

Concrete
633 South Plymouth Court, Suite 208
Chicago, Illinois 60605
Tel: (312) 427-3733
Fax: (312) 427-9503

Cranbrook Academy of Art
1221 North Woodward Avenue,
Box 801
Bloomfield Hills, Michigan 48101
Tel: (801) 645-3336
Fax: (801) 645-3327

Cronan Design
One Zoe Street
San Francisco, California 94107
Tel: (415) 543-6745
Fax: (415) 543-2144

Crosby Associates Inc.
676 North St. Claire, Suite 1805
Chicago, Illinois 60611
Tel: (312) 951-2800
Fax: (312) 951-2814

D•Sign Haus
436 West 47th Street, #4-A
New York, New York 10036
Tel: (212) 548-9111
Fax: (212) 548-5941

Kirk Donnan
655 Corbett Avenue, #506
San Francisco, California 94114
Tel: (415) 282-9827

Donovan and Green
71 Fifth Avenue
New York, New York 10003
Tel: (212) 989-4050
Fax: (212) 989-1453

Drenttel Doyle Partners
1123 Broadway
New York, New York 10010
Tel: (212) 463-8787
Fax: (212) 633-2916

Eric Baker Design Associates
11 East 22nd Street
New York, New York 10010
Tel: (212) 598-9111
Fax: (212) 598-5941

Essex Two
2210 West North Avenue
Chicago, Illinois 60647
Tel: (312) 489-1400
Fax: (312) 489-8422

Feldman Design
2591 Traymore Road
Cleveland, Ohio 44118
Tel: (216) 321-0653
Fax: (216) 321-0653

Grafik Communications Ltd.
1199 North Fairfax Street, Suite 700
Alexandria, Virginia 22314
Tel: (703) 683-4686
Fax: (703) 683-3740

Greteman Group
142 North Mosely, Third Floor
Wichita, Kansas 67202
Tel: (316) 263-1004
Fax: (316) 263-1060

Guggenheim Museum Soho
575 Broadway
New York, New York 10012
Tel: (212) 423-3805
Fax: (212) 966-0903

Harp and Company
48 Olcott Road North
Big Flats, New York 14814
Tel: (607) 562-8681
Fax: (607) 562-3442

Husk Jennings Advertising
50 North Laura Street, Suite 2600
Jacksonville, Florida 32202
Tel: (904) 354-2600
Fax: (904) 354-7226

Rod **J**oslin
14 East Poplar Street
Columbus, Ohio 43215
Tel: (614) 224-8313
Fax: (614) 224-1802

Lamson Design
817 Main Street
Cincinnati, Ohio 45202
Tel: (513) 381-6121
Fax: (513) 381-6122

Leah Lococo
146 East 46th Street
New York, New York 10017
Tel: (212) 682-2921

Liska and Associates, Inc.
676 North St. Clair, Suite 1550
Chicago, Illinois 60611
Tel: (312) 943-4609
Fax: (312) 943-4975

Michael Stanard, Inc.
1000 Main Street
Evanston, Illinois 60202
Tel: (708) 869-9820
Fax: (708) 869-9826

Miho
One Champion Plaza
Stamford, Connecticut 06921
Tel: (818) 396-2351
Fax: (818) 795-0819

Mlicki Design
1847 West Fifth Avenue
Columbus, Ohio 43212
Tel: (614) 486-0286

The Museum of Contemporary Art,
Los Angeles
250 South Grand Avenue
Los Angeles, California 90012
Tel: (213) 621-1724
Fax: (213) 620-8674

Paul Nini
The Ohio State University
380 Hopkins Hall
128 North Oval Mall
Columbus, Ohio 43210
Tel: (614) 292-6746

Pat Taylor, Inc.
3540 South Street, Northwest
Washington, DC 20007
Tel: (202) 338-0962

Patterson Wood Partners
133 West 19th Street
New York, New York 10011
Tel: (212) 691-7734
Fax: (212) 929-3391

Penn State Design Practicomm
210 Patterson Building
University Park, Pennsylvania 16802
Tel: (814) 865-1203
Fax: (814) 863-8664

Pentagram
620 Davis Street
San Francisco, California 94111
Tel: (415) 981-6612
Fax: (415) 981-1826

Pentagram Design
212 Fifth Avenue
New York, New York 10010
Tel: (212) 683-7000
Fax: (212) 532-0181

Pictogram Studio
1740 U Street Northwest, #2
Washington, DC 20009
Tel: (202) 483-4279
Fax: (202) 745-3782

Powell Street Studio
2135 Powell Street
San Francisco, California 94133
Tel: (415) 986-6564
Fax: (415) 397-4765

Rev Visual
690 Sugartown Road
Malvern, Pennsylvania 19355
Tel: (610) 644-4698
Fax: (610) 644-4748

Reverb
5541 Wilshire Boulevard, #900
Los Angeles, California 90036
Tel: (213) 954-4370
Fax: (213) 938-7632

Richard Danne & Associates
126 Fifth Avenue
New York, New York 10011

Tel: (212) 645-7400
Fax: (212) 645-7707

Rigelhaupt Design
18 East 16th Street
New York, New York 10003
Tel: (212) 206-9141
Fax: (212) 929-6284

Riney, Bradford & Huber
735 East Battery Street
San Francisco, California 94111
Tel: (415) 955-4286

Ronn Campisi Design
118 Newbury Street
Boston, Massachusetts 02116
Tel: (671) 236-1339
Fax: (671) 236-0458

Sackett Design Associates
2103 Scott Street
San Francisco, California 94115
Tel: (415) 929-4800
Fax: (415) 929-4819

Schmeltz + Warren
74 Sheffield Road
Columbus, Ohio 43214
Tel: (614) 262-3055

Shapiro Design Associates Inc.
10 East 40th Street
New York, New York 10016
Tel: (212) 685-4095
Fax: (212) 685-3951

Shepard/Quraeshi Associates
501 Heath Street
Chestnut Hills, Massachusetts 02167
Tel: (617) 232-1117
Fax: (617) 232-1411

Kirk Richard Smith
Firehouse 101 Design
492 Armstrong Street
Columbus, Ohio 43215
Tel: (614) 464-0928
Fax: (614) 464-0944

Sommese Design
481 Glenn Road
State College, Pennsylvania 16803
Tel: (814) 238-7484

Step-By-Step Publishing
6000 North Forest Park Drive
Peoria, Illinois 61614
Tel: (309) 688-2300
Fax: (309) 688-8515

Stoltze Design
49 Melcher Street, Fourth Floor
Boston, Massachusetts 02210
Tel: (617) 350-7109
Fax: (617) 482-1171

Studio Morris
55 Vandam Street, Suite 901
New York, New York 10013
Tel: (212) 366-0401
Fax: (212) 366-4101

Tana & Co.
511 Sixth Avenue, Suite 370

New York, New York 10011
Tel: (212) 633-1910
Fax: (212) 655-0219

Tharp Did It
50 University Avenue, Suite 21
Los Gatos, California 95030
Tel: (408) 354-6726
Fax: (408) 354-1450

Total Design
Van Diemenstraat 200
1013 Cp Amsterdam
Tel: (20) 624-7426
Fax: (20) 622-4345

The Traver Company
1601 Second Avenue
Seattle, Washington 98101
Tel: (206) 411-0611
Fax: (206) 728-6016

Victore Design Works
146 East 46th Street
New York, New York 10017
Tel: (212) 682-3734
Fax: (212) 682-2921

Wages Design
1201 West Peachtree Street, #3630
Atlanta, Georgia 30309
Tel: (404) 876-0874

Warner Bros. Records
3300 Warner Boulevard
Burbank, California 91505
Tel: (818) 953-3364
Fax: (818) 953-3232

Wexner Center Design Department
North High Street at 15th Avenue
Columbus, Ohio 43210
Tel: (614) 292-0704
Fax: (614) 291-2955

Whitehouse & Company
18 East 16th Street
New York, New York 10003
Tel: (212) 982-1080
Fax: (212) 727-2150

Clients

Aid Atlanta
1438 Peachtree Street Northwest
Atlanta, Georgia 30309
Tel: (404) 872-0600
Fax: (404) 885-6799

American Express
200 Vesey Street
New York, New York 10285
Tel: (212) 640-5445

American Express Travel Related
Services Company, Inc.
200 Vesey Street
New York, New York 10285

American Institute of Graphic Arts
Chicago Chapter
2210 West North Avenue
Chicago, Illinois 60647
Tel: (312) 489-8424
Fax: (312) 489-8422

American Institute of Graphic Arts
Minnesota Chapter
275 Market Street, Suite 54
Minneapolis, Minnesota 55405
Tel: (612) 339-6904
Fax: (612) 338-7981

American Institute of Graphic Arts
Washington Chapter
3540 South Street Northwest
Washington, DC 20007
Tel: (202) 338-0962
Fax: (202) 337-4102

American Institute of Graphic Arts
Wichita Chapter
Post Office Box 2612
Wichita, Kansas 67201

American Museum of the
Moving Image
3601 35th Avenue
Astoria, New York 11106
Tel: (718) 784-0077
Fax: (718) 784-4681

American-Standard
1114 Avenue of the Americas
New York, New York 10036
Tel: (212) 703-5379
Fax: (212) 703-5352

Ameritech Corporation
30 South Wacker Drive
Chicago, Illinois 60606
Tel: (312) 750-5000
Fax: (312) 207-1601

Art Center College of Design
(See Design Firms)

The Art Directors Club, Inc.
250 Paniark Avenue South
New York, New York 10003
Tel: (212) 674-0500
Fax: (212) 228-0649

The Art Museum, Princeton University
Princeton, New Jersey 08544
Tel: (609) 258-4341
Fax: (609) 258-5949

AT&T
1605 Inwood Terrace
Jacksonville, Florida 32207
Tel: (904) 396-7945

The Barnes Foundation
300 North Latch's Lane
Merion, Pennsylvania 19066
Tel: (215) 667-0290
Fax: (215) 644-4026

Bellas Artes International
341 Benton Street
Santa Rosa, California 95401
Tel: (707) 573-3701
Fax: (707) 573-3701

Booz•Allen & Hamilton Inc.
8283 Greensboro Drive
McLean, Virginia 22101
Tel: (703) 902-5559
Fax: (703) 902-3389

Boston Ballet
19 Clarendon Street
Boston, Massachusetts 02116
Tel: (671) 695-6950
Fax: (671) 695-6995

The Brooklyn Children's Museum
145 Brooklyn Avenue
Brooklyn, New York 11213
Tel: (718) 735-4444
Fax: (718) 604-7442

California Institute of the Arts
24700 McBean Parkway
Valencia, California 91355
Tel: (805) 253-7832
Fax: (805) 255-2894

The Center for Children and Families
295 Lafayette Street
New York, New York 10012
Tel: (212) 226-8536
Fax: (212) 226-1918

Champion International Corp.
One Champion Plaza
Stamford, Connecticut 06921
Tel: (818) 577-9015

Chase Manhattan
One Chase Plaza
New York, New York 10081
Tel: (212) 552-7678

City of Leewarden
Raad Huis Plein 36
Leewarden, Friesland 8900ja
The Netherlands
Tel: (58) 924-200

The Cleveland Clinic Foundation
9500 Euclid Avenue
Cleveland, Ohio 44195
Tel: (216) 444-2496
Fax: (216) 444-8256

Coalition for the Homeless
89 Chambers Street
New York, New York 10007
Tel: (212) 964-5900
Fax: (212) 695-8331

The Contemporary Arts Center
115 East Fifth Street
Cincinnati, Ohio 45202
Tel: (513) 345-8400
Fax: (513) 721-7418

Cranbrook Academy of Art
(See Design Firms)

Cronan Artefact
11 Zoe Street
San Francisco, California 94107
Tel: (415) 543-3387
Fax: (415) 543-4482

Dallas Society of Visual
Communications
3530 High Mesa
Dallas, Texas 75234
Tel: (214) 241-2017
Fax: (214) 247-8735

Ernst & Young
787 Seventh Avenue
New York, New York 10019
Tel: (212) 773-5698
Fax: (212) 773-5055

Fashion Institute of Technology
7th Avenue at 27th Street
New York, New York 10001
Tel: (212) 760-7642

Federal Reserve Bank of Chicago
230 South LaSalle Street
Chicago, Illinois 60604
Tel: (312) 322-8380
Fax: (312) 322-5332

The Franklin Institute
Science Museum
222 North 20th Street
Philadelphia, Pennsylvania 19103
Tel: (215) 448-1129
Fax: (215) 448-1235

General Foods USA
250 North Street
White Plains, New York 10625
Tel: (914) 335-2480

Goethe House
1014 Fifth Avenue
New York, New York 10028
Tel: (212) 439-8700
Fax: (212) 439-8705

Hallmark/Creative Resource Division
2501 McGee
Kansas City, Missouri 64141
Tel: (800) 821-2118
Fax: (816) 274-7245

Haworth, Inc.
One Haworth Center
Holland, Michigan 49423
Tel: (616) 393-3000

Hexcel
5794 West Las Positas Boulevard
Pleasanton, California 94588
Tel: (510) 847-9500

Homart
55 West Monroe, Suite 3100
Chicago, Illinois 60603
Tel: (312) 551-5000
Fax: (312) 551-5484

Illinois Institute of Technology
3200 South Wabash Avenue
Chicago, Illinois 60616
Tel: (312) 567-3106

Inova Health System
8001 Braddock Road
Springfield, Virginia 22151
Tel: (703) 321-4338
Fax: (703) 321-4219

Isabella Stewart Gardner Museum
Two Palace Road
Boston, Massachusetts 02115
Tel: (617) 566-1401
Fax: (617) 232-8039

The **J.** Paul Getty Museum
17985 Pacific Coast Highway
Malibu, CA 90265
Tel: (310) 459-7611
Fax: (310) 454-8156

Jake's Attic
Post Office Box 781714
Wichita, Kansas 67278
Tel: (316) 685-3955

Knoll Group
105 Wooster Street
New York, New York 10012
Tel: (212) 343-4160

KPMG Peat Marwick
767 Fifth Avenue
New York, New York 10153
Tel: (212) 909-5000

KPMG Peat Marwick
Three Chestnut Ridge Road
Montvale, New Jersey 07645
Tel: (201) 307-7277
Fax: (201) 307-7703

Learning International
225 High Ridge Road
Stamford, Connecticut 06904
Tel: (203) 965-8400

Lincoln Center Productions
70 Lincoln Center Plaza
New York, New York 10023
Tel: (212) 875-5384
Fax: (212) 875-5414

Little Red School House &
Elisabeth Irwin High School
196 Bleeker Street
New York, New York 10012
Tel: (212) 477-5316
Fax: (212) 677-9159

Marathon Shopping Centers Group
One Galleria Tower
13355 Noel Road, #1200
Dallas, Texas 75240
Tel: (214) 458-1200
Fax: (214) 458-7619

Massachusetts Institute of Technology
77 Massachusetts Avenue, #3-108
Cambridge, Massachusetts 02139
Tel: (617) 253-1000
Fax: (617) 258-8304

Methodist Hospital of Indiana
Post Office Box 1367
Indianapolis, Indiana 46206
Tel: (317) 929-2000

Michael Stanard, Inc.
(See Design Firms)

MTV Networks
1515 Broadway
New York, New York 10036
Tel: (212) 258-8795
Fax: (212) 258-6481

The Museum of Contemporary Art,
Los Angeles
(See Design Firms)

The Museum of Contemporary Art,
San Diego
700 Prospect Street
La Jolla, California 92037
Tel: (691) 234-1001

Museum of Jewish Heritage
342 Madison Avenue
New York, New York 10173
Tel: (212) 687-9141

National Design Museum,
Smithsonian Institution
Two East 91st Street
New York, New York 10128
Tel: (212) 860-6868

New York City Deptartment of
Environmental Protection
59-17 Junction Boulevard
Corona, New York 11368
Tel: (718) 595-3482
Fax: (718) 595-3477

New York Times Company
229 West 43rd Street
New York, New York 10036
Tel: (212) 556-1655

Olympia and York Companies
200 Liberty Street, Second Floor
New York, New York 10281
Tel: (212) 945-2600

Penn State Department of
Landscape Architecture
210 Engineering, Unit D
University Park, Pennsylvania 16802
Tel: (814) 865-9511

Penn State School of Visual Arts
210 Patterson Building
University Park, Pennsylvania 16802
Tel: (814) 238-7484
Fax: (814) 863-8664

Pentagram Design
(See Design Firms)

Phamis, Inc.
401 Second Avenue South, Suite 200
Seattle, Washington 98104
Tel: (206) 622-9558
Fax: (206) 622-0889

Prudential Home Mortgage
343 Thornall Street
Edison, New Jersey 08837
Tel: (908) 906-5800
Fax: (908) 906-3904

San Francisco Museum of
Modern Art
151 Third Street
San Francisco, California 94103
Tel: (415) 357-4000
Fax: (415) 357-4037

San Francisco Zoological Society
One Zoo Road
San Francisco, California 94132

San Jose Museum of Art
10 South Market Street
San Jose, California 95113

Tel: (408) 294-2787
Fax: (408) 294-2977

Saturn Corporation
100 Saturn Parkway
Spring Hill, Tennessee 37174
Tel: (615) 486-5055
Fax: (615) 486-5059

Shearson Lehman Brothers
World Financial Center, 20th Floor
New York, New York 10285
Tel: (212) 640-5445

Smithsonian Institution
1001 Jefferson Drive
Southwest, #3146
Washington, DC 20560
Tel: (202) 357-3208
Fax: (202) 357-4324

Society for Environmental
Graphic Design
One Story Street
Cambridge, Massachusetts 02138
Tel: (617) 868-3381
Fax: (617) 868-3591

Software Components Group
731 Technology Drive, Suite 300
San Jose, California 95110
Tel: (202) 775-0333
Fax: (202) 775-0402

Solomon R. Guggenheim Museum
1071 Fifth Avenue
New York, New York 10128
Tel: (212) 423-3533
Fax: (212) 423-3650

Step-By-Step Publishing,
(See Design Firms)

Synoptics Communications, Inc.
4401 Great American Parkway
Santa Clara, California 95052

Time Warner, Inc.
75 Rockefeller Plaza, 14th Floor
New York, New York 10019
Fax: (212) 275-3970

United Way of New York City
99 Park Avenue
New York, New York 10016
Tel: (212) 973-3900
Fax: (212) 661-1990

University of California, San Diego
School of Architecture
9500 Gilman Drive
La Jolla, California 92093
Tel: (619) 534-0639
Fax: (619) 534-0298

Warner Bros. Records
(See Design Firms)

Western Art Directors Club
Post Office Box 996
Palo Alto, California 94302
Tel: (415) 321-4196

Wexner Center for the Arts
(See Design Firms)

Index

The authors wish to thank Deby Harding, our editor at PBC, for her timeless efforts on behalf of this project. Thanks also to Mark Serchuck, publisher; Penny Sibal, managing director; Susan Kapsis, managing editor; Richard Liu, technical director; Frank Zanone; Alyson Heegan and Dorene Evans for all their support and encouragement. Gratitude to Mirko Ilić, designer, for his exceptional work and Naum Kazhdan for additional photography. Finally much thanks to the contributors without whom this book would be blank.